The Leadership Mind Switch pushed me to forge my own thoughts on leading across generations—and to act now.

> **—Amy Carney**, President, Research and Advertiser Sales at
> Sony Picture Television

The Leadership Mind Switch is not another book about leadership. It tells the story of how technology combined with cultural and generational demographics are changing the work environment more rapidly than society has ever seen. The fourth revolution is quickly becoming our business reality. *The Leadership Mind Switch* will help you understand the dynamics of the changes and how to evolve as a leader.

> **—Clare Hart**, CEO of Sterling Talent Solutions

The Leadership Mind Switch is the most comprehensive manual I have seen in preparing the leaders of yesterday to be the leaders of tomorrow. Truly a MUST-READ for any executive in any industry!

> **—Rulon F. Stacey**, PhD, FACHE, Chair, Board of Overseers at
> Malcolm Baldrige National Quality Award and Managing Director
> of Navigant Consulting

This is simply an outstanding book on leadership! It is conceptually deep, yet is highly pragmatic in its approach. This book is going to be a steady North Star for leaders as they navigate the fast changing landscape of virtually everything they need to manage and manage through.

> **—Raja Rajamannar**, Global Chief Marketing & Communications Officer
> and President of Healthcare Division at Mastercard

The Leadership Mind Switch provides the tools and insights for aspiring leaders.

> **—Kazu Gomi**, CEO and President at NTT America, Inc.

This book is a perfect toolbox for both aspiring and existing leaders. Debra Benton and Kylie Wright-Ford suggest a fact and real-life experience-based, concrete, practical approach to revisiting one's skill set—based on facts and real-life experiences. They gradually bring the reader into a new and more complex leadership environment while taking away any anxiety and replacing it with the idea that all these new "issues" are in reality "opportunities" for a more effective and rewarding leadership style.

> **—Andrea Ragnetti**, member of Board at TEKA GROUP and
> Former CEO of Alitalia

What's keeping you from reading *The Leadership Mind Switch* right now? We all know leadership is at the heart of great movements in science, business, technology, and politics. The thoughtful and provocative ideas raised in this book will switch you on.

> **—Scott Goodson**, CEO of StrawberryFrog and bestselling author
> of *Uprising*

Last year's technological frontier already looks small in the rearview mirror, and demographics are rapidly changing as well. Both bring fantastic opportunities and daunting challenges. Benton and Wright-Ford show us how to realize the first and overcome the second with the kind of wisdom that can't be found using search engines.

> **—Dino Falaschetti**, PhD, MBA, Chief Economist of U.S. House Committee on Financial Services

The Leadership Mind Switch offers leaders a fresh and practical approach to navigating the evolving complexities of the fourth industrial revolution. After reading the experienced perspective and wisdom of Benton and Wright-Ford, rising and seasoned leaders will be able to go to work with the critical skills they need to be ready for the future.

> **—Rick Ambrose**, Executive Vice President at Lockheed Martin Corporation and President of Space Systems Company

As the CEO of a disruptive industrial 3D printing company, I couldn't agree more that technology and demographics have changed everything for us—and our leadership needs to catch up! A must-read for both aspirational and practical guidelines to the new world of work.

> **—Rick Smith**, CEO of Fast Radius and founder and former CEO of World50 and of G100 Next Leadership

The world is changing fast, but many of our leadership models are stuck in the past. Based on years of experience, Debra and Kylie have written a book that addresses the leadership needs challenges of today and tomorrow. It not only recognizes the warp speed changes in technology but also very deep emotional needs that people still have.

> **—Daryl Brewster**, CEO of Committee Encouraging Corporate Philanthropy (CECP)

I could feel the energy literally jumping off the pages of *The Leadership Mind Switch*. This book clearly presents the future landscape of how people and technology will intersect with opportunities. Benton and Wright-Ford show us how to navigate successfully through this challenging new crossroads of people, work, technology, and leadership.

> **—Paul Schlossberg**, President of DFW Consulting

In a recent address to a group of employees, I said, "Our customer of the future is someone like my 21-year-old daughter. They think, work, and communicate in a whole different realm, and we need to adapt our service to their needs in a differentiated way." Debra and Kylie's book strikes at the heart of this exact issue. Everyone on my leadership team will receive a copy to read.

> **—Barbara Smith**, President of Commercial Metals Company

For both "rising leaders" and "nimble masters," this is a great practical guide for successfully meeting the complex challenges presented by globalization, unimaginable technological change, and generational diversity in the workplace

> **—M. Carl Johnson, III**, Chairman of the Board at Nautilus, Inc. and 2017 Fellow, Distinguished Careers Institute, Stanford University

A must-read for the experienced as well as the aspiring leader during this time of unprecedented pace of change.

> **—Uta Werner**, Chief Strategy Officer at Signet

The world has changed. Successful business management requires leadership innovation at all levels from the frontline manager to the CEO. Applying the principles outlined in this book will enable leaders to make the mind switch necessary to be successful. A great read!

> **—Mike Dennison**, President of Flex Inc.

The Leadership Mind Switch is a refreshingly modern, in-your-face view of leadership that explains how technology is erasing the generation gap and crystalizes the mindsets and behaviors key to becoming a "fourth revolution leader.'

> **—Joe Spagnoletti**, former CIO of Campbell Soup Company and founder of Spagnoletti Net.

In a world syncopated by split-seconds and nanotechnology, we all need a mind shift to lead. Rather than top-down commands, Benton and Wright-Ford show us that the best leadership tools are continuous learning, constant engagement, and the ability to inspire.

> **—Mike Fernandez**, CEO-U.S. of Burson-Marsteller

The next 10 years will bring technological and demographic changes that will continue to revolutionize the workplace. As leaders, we need to change our mindset in order to seize new opportunities. In *The Leadership Mind Switch*, Debra Benton and Kylie Wright-Ford provide practical advice on how to lead and succeed in this environment.

> **—Deanna Mulligan**, President and CEO of The Guardian Life Insurance Company of America

THE LEADERSHIP MIND SWITCH

RETHINKING HOW WE LEAD IN THE NEW WORLD OF WORK

D. A. BENTON
KYLIE WRIGHT-FORD

New York Chicago San Francisco Athens London Madrid
Mexico City Milan New Delhi Singapore Sydney Toronto

1 2 3 4 5 6 7 8 9   LCR   22 21 20 19 18 17

ISBN   978-1-259-83604-6
MHID   1-259-83604-5

e-ISBN   978-1-259-83605-3
e-MHID   1-259-83605-3

Library of Congress Cataloging-in-Publication Data
Names: Benton, D. A. (Debra A.), author. | Ford-Wright, Kylie, author.
Title: The leadership mind switch : rethinking how we lead in the new
    world of work / D.A. Benton and Kylie Ford-Wright.
Description: New York : McGraw-Hill, [2017]
Identifiers: LCCN 2016055005 (print) | LCCN 2017013972 (ebook) | ISBN
    9781259836053 () | ISBN 1259836053 () | ISBN 9781259836046 (alk.
    paper) | ISBN 1259836045
Subjects: LCSH: Leadership.
Classification: LCC HD57.7 (ebook) | LCC HD57.7 .B4668 2017 (print) |
    DDC 658.4/092--dc23
LC record available at https://lccn.loc.gov/2016055005

McGraw-Hill Education books are available at special quantity discounts
to use as premiums and sales promotions or for use in corporate training
programs. To contact a representative, please visit the Contact Us pages at
www.mhprofessional.com.

. . . for both you "rising leaders" and "masters of leadership":

If you are keen on forging your own distinctive style of leadership in today's business world, then you have picked up the right book. We have entered an era of unprecedented change, driven by shifting demographics and advancing technologies—a time in which the ability to skillfully lead a multigenerational workforce is paramount. You probably sense this shifting tide in the workplace as it makes our jobs more challenging, but also more exciting. It is being called the fourth industrial revolution, and it is going to be big.

The Leadership Mind Switch is meant for readers who see opportunities where many others see boundaries; for both experienced leaders who want to stay relevant longer and rising leaders seeking guidance for their future, all of whom want to create positivity and make better decisions in the world—and for the world.

—D. A. (Debra) and Kylie

Contents

THE FOURTH INDUSTRIAL REVOLUTION

> *The factory of the future will have only two employees, a man and a dog. The man will be there to feed the dog. The dog will be there to keep the man from touching the equipment.*
>
> —WARREN BENNIS

As you pick up this book, you may be experiencing a shift in your workplace, in your organization, or even in your professional lifestyle as the world around you changes rapidly. Perhaps you are reaching a new stage in your career and wrestling with how to be successful going forward. Maybe you are building your leadership skills or trying to refine them to fit the current needs of your team.

The books you read and the advice you receive on leadership are probably from another era, one of iconic business, political, or historical leaders. Some of this advice is certainly still relevant, but some is entirely antiquated—the leadership game has changed substantially over time, even in the last two years, and continues to do so.

We wrote *The Leadership Mind Switch* to help you thrive in this new business landscape, what is being called the fourth industrial revolution. Unveiled by global thinkers at the 2016 World Economic Forum, this revolution is set to transform the way we need to lead and live.

A NOTE TO OUR READERS

Throughout the book, you will see quotes from conversations we have had with leaders on various subjects. These words of wisdom come directly from leaders of all ages and walks of life and represent their current thinking. We found that these tiny pieces of insight reflect the hundreds of people we talked to about the leadership mind switch and why it is needed. You will also find "Stories from the Road" at the end of each chapter. They too reflect the diversity of the leaders we interviewed— from Fortune 500 leaders to MBA students. You will find a story from a global CMO, a CFO at a private equity firm, presidents and academics, millennials and sage advisors, even a couple who bought a whole town! We want you to relate to different stories in different ways. This is part of the point of the mind switch that is needed—leadership is not about a title, it is about the qualities and behaviors that you exude. And nuggets of how to succeed can come from many different corners in the diverse world we live in.

Leaders mostly rely on habits and processes that have served them well in the past—we use our wisdom to guide us, and it is an efficient way to behave. However, the premise for this book, and our firm belief, is that a mind switch is needed now to be ready for the future. When the environment changes dramatically, which it has and will continue to do as the fourth revolution unfolds, actions and thoughts need to adjust similarly. The leadership mind switch portrays a radical change to the way you think about your leadership behaviors and qualities. It is more than a shift in your mindset. It is a jolt to the way you think and act. The urgency to change is based on a realization that moving at the pace of the past is not going to work effectively any more—especially when leading across different generations and styles.

Before we dive into the mind switch in detail, perhaps some background to the way our workforce has evolved will give context. Many of us are a little rusty on the history of the first three eras of industry—the so-called revolutions.

The first industrial revolution was characterized by the transition from old to new manufacturing processes; the second by a technological phase of rapid industrialization and mass production; and the third by the digitization of manufacturing. In the words of the World Economic Forum, the "fourth industrial revolution" "is characterized by a fusion of technologies that is blurring the lines between the physical, digital, and biological spheres." To us, it is a collective term describing contemporary automation, digital data exchange, and new manufacturing technologies, such as the blending of robots, virtual reality, and the "to be determined"! This is both exciting and confusing.

Your organization may be moving faster or slower than the average workplace, but you will need to be ready for anything if you want to stay relevant and impactful. The future will be vastly different, with changes happening at warp speed—you're way past the "rat race," this is more like the "gazelle race." It is going to be a new world of work, and as a leader, you will need to operate with an urgency you have never felt before. You may have seen the stats: 50 percent of the workforce will be between the ages of 20 and 40 years old by 2020. That means your bosses, colleagues, employees, customers, and competitors will look and behave differently than they do now.

As one of our good friends, Scott Goodson, founder and CEO of StrawberryFrog and author of *Uprising*, says, "Leading right now is kind of like you have a machete strapped to your chest, your safari suit on, and are charging into the jungle." We like this analogy because it captures the raw nature of the reality and, for most of us, the foreign environment that we are entering amid changing technologies and demographics.

«‹›»

The Leadership Mind Switch gives you the tools and information that you will need to be fulfilled, happy, and impactful as these shifts gather pace. Because expectations, requirements, and demands have been changed, we want to help you make a mind switch so you can lead across generations (from boomers to Gen X, Gen Y, and Gen Z), utilizing different leadership styles and transforming the way you inspire others in the future.

The two authors of this book have backgrounds as an executive coach and a contemporary executive. We live and work with new leadership demands every day and have personally experienced the lightning-speed changes in technological innovation and demographic disruption that are currently occurring. We have watched some leaders struggle and others thrive.

Executive coach D. A. (Debra) Benton has over 35 years of experience consulting with Fortune 500 executives, Silicon Valley start-ups, and entrepreneurs in 18 different countries; speaking and coaching on persuasive leadership communication skills; writing articles and popular blogs, and publishing bestselling business books. Kylie Wright-Ford is an Australian-born operating executive, entrepreneur, speaker, and guest lecturer on leadership. She was most recently the chief operating and strategy officer of World 50, is a Goldman Sachs (JBWere) alum, and Oxford MBA. She has lived and worked on three different continents and currently lives in the United States.

We lead, manage, coach, and advise people living with the new workplace dynamics, providing our experienced perspectives through our global, firsthand knowledge and leadership backgrounds. Together we produce the kind of wisdom that can't be found using search engines. Like you, we wanted to know what's needed to succeed going forward, and through writing this book, we've found answers to help all of us lead into the future.

As a recent Apple advertising campaign proclaims, "The only thing that's changed is *everything*." So let's get started.

Welcome to *The Leadership Mind Switch*!

Please visit our websites:
www.makethemindswitch.com
www.debrabenton.com
www.kyliewf.com

PART ONE

Leading Today and Tomorrow

Really good leaders are needed now more than ever.

Leadership methods that worked in the past won't work going forward. Leading in the future will require fresh thinking in both practice and behavior. Good leaders will have to be more agile and enlightened than their predecessors, operate with transparency and tenacity, and be more honest and communicative. They will need the skills to understand, relate to, and work with people of all kinds, regardless of their age, background, or individual idiosyncrasies.

The urgency around being such a leader has skyrocketed. During the next 10 years we will experience an unprecedented storm of technological and demographic shifts. This storm will sweep in remarkable changes in the way we interact with each other, our devices, and the world around us, while also presenting new, unmatched opportunities.

A metamorphosis is under way. In a world where the dividing lines between humans and machines are becoming gray, how we respond to this revolution as leaders, and develop our uniquely human skills, will be determined solely by our actions.

In the words of Klaus Schwab, founder of the World Economic Forum in Davos, "I believe we need to emphasize the more human aspect in leadership as a counterweight to all of these technological changes" (*Time* magazine, January 2016). And this is true. Bringing your whole self to work and inspiring others through your behavior is more important now than ever before.

> **"Really good leaders are needed now more than ever."**

Despite all of the changes that we are experiencing, however, there are two things that have stayed consistent:

1. **Leadership is everything in business.** A quality person has to confidently step up and take the lead, set an example, chart the course, and provide feedback. In other words, leaders still need to get people to do what they want them to do, while keeping them happy and productive.

2. **Someone is going to take the lead, and it might as well be you.** Whether you've just entered into a managerial role or you've been a CEO for years, you have the ability to harness the new opportunities presented by today's exciting new challenges. This is not a time to idly sit by—it is a time when fortune will *truly* favor the brave.

THE CHANGING WORLD OF LEADERSHIP

While human brain size has remained largely the same for the last few centuries, we have massively accelerated the way we collect and consume information. Speaking at a recent Techonomy conference, Eric Schmidt, former CEO of Google, said, "Every two days we create as much information as we did from the dawn of man through 2003." This rapid expansion of available information has both welcome and unwelcome consequences. We are better informed today than probably ever before, but the sheer amount of facts, figures, and opinions that constantly bombard us can be overwhelming.

Similarly, technology seems to be ever expanding. Consider that, before long, your work headquarters will likely have robots on staff. Remote employees and telecommuters may control them from the comfort of their own homes no matter where they live, using them to attend meetings more visibly and collaborate more effectively. Don't be surprised if you see one wearing a toupee rolling down the hall—robots are sort of people, too!

Maybe it sounds far-fetched, but think of the new advances that have already helped you collaborate and bridge both time and distance in the global workplace. Skype and FaceTime, for example, were major developments in communication methods, but they will prove to be only the tip of the iceberg.

The ability to communicate with ease from almost anywhere in the world has also reshaped the traditional role of the office. Physical office dynamics have changed dramatically for many Fortune 500 leaders. More than one of the chief executives we interviewed for this book claims to have a "window office"—a window *seat* in the bulkhead of a plane where they spend time between business meetings and customer visits. In recent years, many leaders don't even have a desk because they firmly believe that an open door is not enough to stay connected to their team—they literally use their mobile phone as their office and move around the workspace, and sometimes the world, according to their schedule that day.

Leadership today is about character and communication, not corner offices. Each year we collectively speak to hundreds of leaders who are embracing open plan seating and the idea of "being with their people." They do so to connect with their teams and exhibit their authenticity, an idea that is being retooled in the workplace as well. Gone are the days where leaders are expected to be infallible, perfect, and remote. Now, some leaders are even playful in the workplace to model their willingness to try new things and bring levity to a demanding environment. Not only are they connecting differently with their current teams, but they are also experiencing drastic changes in how they attract new talent.

Potential employees today have certain expectations when it comes to the workplace, which we believe has resulted in a shift of power from the hiring company to the job seeker. For instance, think about the campuses in Silicon Valley. The way in which they operate and use technology to enable collaboration has completely evolved. They use open floor plans, creative

> **"Once people get used to the idea that you are always present even if you are not in one place, the major barriers to communication start to come down."**

titles, a variety of communication tools, flexible work schedules, and some other rather lavish perks to keep employees healthy and comfortable with their work-life balance. Some of these additional perks that are slowly becoming the norm are shown below.

- » Meditation rooms and exercise classes or gym memberships
- » Healthy food trucks in the office parking lot
- » Free food
- » Parking lot car washing and gassing
- » Bike repair
- » Transportation allowance
- » Same-day laundry service
- » Haircuts and custom tailoring
- » Car repair, dry cleaning, and minor medical services on site

» Relaxed rules around dress, visible tattoos, and facial hair

» Required sabbaticals

» Mandates that you take the day off on your birthday and get a cake upon your return

» Office parties to celebrate anything

» Beer on tap

» Interest-free loans

» Desk swaps to sit somewhere else

» Coworking spaces to foster community

» Company field trips to fun or exotic places

» Bonus cash for new baby

» Game arcades and music jam rooms

» Vacation cash to spend on the road

» Nap pods

» Allowing pets in the office

» Concierge service

» Twice-monthly home housecleaning by corporate janitorial staff

» Creating one's own title, e.g., Job Captain/Finance, not Chief Financial Officer; CEO or Chief Encouragement Officer, Chief Happiness Officer

» Emphasizing wellness with yoga rooms, standing desks, and indoor walking tracks

» Creating their own management programs to develop their talent

» Notifying workers to stop and take a companywide exercise break or food break

» Company rooftop community gardens and concert venues

» Rotating every month where the most inexperienced and most experienced employees do some project together

» Education reimbursements
» Charity of your choice donation matching programs

While all of these perks will help you attract talent, actually keeping your employees engaged is in your hands. All of the plentiful perks in the world will not offset working for a lousy leader.

According to McKinsey & Company, we are experiencing 10 times the pace of change of the first revolution and 300 times the scale. What hasn't changed is that people still work for a person, *not* a company. As a great leader, *you* want to be the one that the "best of the best" want to work *for*, irrespective of the free food in the cafeteria and the quality craft beer on tap. To become such a leader, you need to be intimately knowledgeable about how these changes are impacting both your role and the business environment as a whole. Let's take a closer look at the two major components that are having widespread effects on leaders in the twenty-first century: technology and demographics.

Technology

The ubiquity of technology in our lives can be seen in the way we interact with each other and the companies that dominate our markets. At the time this book is being written, Apple, Alphabet, and Microsoft are the top three most valuable companies listed on the U.S. stock market. Facebook is number 7, and Amazon is number 9.

Today, we use Twitter to exchange ideas; Fitbit to manage our health; Amazon Prime to purchase everything from an iPod to bulk toilet paper; Uber and Lyft to get us around the

> "Looking back, the movie and TV screens we use today will be seen as an intermediate step between the invention of electricity and the invention of VR. Kids will think it's funny that their ancestors used to stare at glowing rectangles hoping to suspend disbelief."

city; and Snapchat, Facebook, and many more to connect with others. We order our food on Gobble and Blue Apron when we are too busy to prepare and cook and even outsource waiting in line for concert tickets on sites like Task-Rabbit. Incrementally life-changing technologies are an everyday occurrence—and that's good. Technology conducts your trains, flies your planes, cures disease, increases crop production, decreases traffic accidents, keeps you safe, cooks your dinner, sets your alarms, keeps track of your children, and organizes and informs you.

Mobile devices alone have been a major game changer in how we live and work together. The average U.S. adult is expected to use his or her mobile device for 5 hours and 56 minutes per day by 2017 (according to eMarketer in October 2015). Back in 2011, the same adults used their mobile devices for just 46 minutes per day.

We also see emerging new technology genres such as virtual reality, machine learning and automation, and the Internet of Things (estimated by International Data Corporation (IDC) growing in size from $655.8 billion in 2014 to $1.7 trillion by 2020)—all of which will surely bring about even greater developments in our everyday lives, just as all major disruptions in technology tend to do.

Technological workplace developments can be daunting. There are leaders who remember a time when lettered mail was delivered at 9:30 a.m. by someone pushing a cart from desk to desk, placed into a real (not figurative) inbox (and outbox). Compare this system to how young adults under 21 years old use images, emoticons, and abbreviations to talk to each other, as if it were second nature. The fusion of technologies, blurring the lines between physical, digital, and biological spheres, has irreversibly changed the way we communicate, manage our careers, lead others, and live.

How Technology Affects Your Job and Career

The way we manage our careers has been dramatically improved by technologies that make the world feel small. We are more informed and empowered than ever to change our jobs, look for higher paying opportunities, and find roles that are more fulfilling, with companies that offer better rewards and the chance to make an impact on the world. Finding these positions can be a few clicks, or a few connections, away. Networking is technically easier than ever with platforms like LinkedIn, XING, and Viadeo, which change the way we keep in touch with coworkers, colleagues, and friends.

The talent pool is larger and more diverse than it's ever been, and the dynamic talent markets in which we operate are far afield for some slow-moving Fortune 500 companies. Innovators are embracing and adapting new technologies. Apps are now the way that we consume, transact, and make career choices. The best companies know this—they develop properties to engage and intrigue current employees and potential candidates (not to mention their customers!).

Technological advances have also expanded workforce participation. You can join the business world earlier—think of students who might be developing apps while still in high school. You can also stay in the game longer: physical workplaces are less important now than ever before, which means seniors are technically less isolated and more able to participate, even if they're providing consultation services from their homes in the Bahamas (we should all be so lucky!). In fact, in a recent survey of Silicon Valley leaders, published in *Atlantic* in November 2016, 20 percent of the panel believed that by 2020 more white-collar Americans will telecommute than work in their offices.

Not only does technology affect how you find new positions, or how companies find you, it also affects the *type* of positions and businesses that are now being developed. The "start-up" is the new titan of industry. There are also countless new short-lived, bedroom-spawned businesses, what Futurist David Zach calls pop-up businesses.

"Pop-up businesses" are created when people tackle a specific project, satisfy a certain need, and then disassemble and disband to move on to another project. If they grow, they are likely funded with crowdsourcing and staffed by flexible workers found on Elance or other sites that specialize in gig-economy converts, those workers who take on temporary positions for shorter periods.

Such developments in the landscape for work necessitate dramatic change in the way leaders need to think about career management for themselves and those they are trying to attract to work for them. This environment has also changed the way we can accelerate our careers as leaders. Consider what you want out of your career: Are you interested in a more traditional business path? Do you want to work for a "time-tested" organization, or are you willing to take a risk on a new venture that may be more exciting or innovative? Once you're in a leadership role, consider what your prospective employees might want out of their careers, too. And think about whether the company you choose to lead within will be well placed to withstand the tech changes and even thrive in them.

Globalization

The pace of globalization—the interaction of people, culture, and trade across different nations—has been accelerated by technology and is now part of everyday life for most professionals around the world. Globalization has an equally long list of pros and cons according to the academics, economists, and pundits that specialize in commenting on global trends, but as it relates to the texture of the workforce, our view is that it is overwhelmingly positive.

With globalization comes a more diverse mosaic of views and perspectives that weren't previously available or relatively affordable to access. Increasingly, our economic and cultural worlds are being intertwined with both those of our geographic neighbors and those that are half way around the world.

For example, we were recently in China with a colleague who is Chinese born, lives in the United States, and is fluent in French. She switches easily between French, Chinese, and English, and her children are trilingual. Her husband is French, and she has a PhD in strategy. This colleague is exactly the type of talent necessary for the fourth revolution!

Traveling in China with her was exhilarating—new technologies are being adopted and businesses are maturing at an incredible speed. China is jumping the curb by learning the best of Western business processes while accessing the better tech infrastructure at their fingertips. One of the clients we visited said to us, "In China, you need to live with a suitcase packed all the time," referencing the fact that the pace of change can be faster in some areas than in the Western world and strategy could shift overnight—you need to respond wherever in the world these better ideas are being developed.

Consider below some recent transactions that speak to the nature of the world we operate within as leaders. Gone are the days of thinking that you can live a domestic life that is untouched by foreign influence.

MIND SWITCH FACTS

» Hollywood film studio Legendary Entertainment was purchased by Asia's richest man.

» Starbucks plans to increase its footprint in China to 5,000 cafés by 2021.

» Russian business tycoon Mikhail Prokhorov's company Onexim Group controls 100 percent of the American basketball team the Brooklyn Nets and Barclays Center.

» Chinese appliance maker Haier bought GE's appliance unit for $5.4 billion.

» The biggest foreign investor of U.S. shale is Australian mining group BHP Billiton.

» Afghanistan won approval to join the World Trade Organization.

Source: Quartz daily brief Qz.com

Our industries, economies, and workforce are more vibrant and globally minded than ever, and with the rapid growth of technology, this trend is set to continue. Take for example just one factor: the languages people speak. An August 2013 U.S. Census report from 2009 to 2013 found that 60 million Americans speak languages other than English at home (some 300-plus different languages).

> **"Frankly, leading and managing today is like dealing with a box full of puppies."**

For example:

New York = 192 different languages
San Francisco = 163 different languages
Dallas = 156 different languages

In addition to the more common German, French, Spanish, Italian, Vietnamese, Korean, and Chinese, you have Havasupi, Swahili, Onondaga, Bengali, Picuris, Hindi, Tungus, Hawaiian, Bengali, Pima, Amharic, Serbian, Tamil, Indonesian, Malayalan, Kiowa, Pidgin, Croatian, French Creole, Samoan, and Mandarin, which is just a small sample.

MIND SWITCH FACTS

Pew Research Center points out that the number of multinational Americans is on the rise, growing three times as fast as the country's population as a whole.

And with different languages come varying customs, beliefs, hygiene, dress, food, manner, comportment, and history. These divergent backgrounds mean the requirement for open-mindedness and the ability to lead across varied styles is more important than ever. Communication competencies and willingness to learn are also heightened needs for the fourth revolution leader.

Although every generation thinks its workplace texture is unlike any before, it's really true now. We have a workforce unlike any we've had previously, with people all over the world from disparate backgrounds, fueled by unbelievable technology and resulting in amazing diversity. If you are finding it hard to keep up, you are in good company, but you must be willing to continually learn and adapt to this new world. It is a tough but stimulating landscape where, in the words of one entrepreneur we spoke to, "Pretty much you can be the disrupter or you can be the disrupted. It's your choice."

Leading with Technology

All of these new technologies have transformed the way we must lead. The adoption of workplace tools that enable easier organization across global teams, our ability to influence others through online communication, and the way we work together are unlike anything that has come before.

Technology is a tool, a utensil, a gadget, an instrument, and a device. As a leader, you must use this tool. Whether it be FaceTime to gather ideas from a team member in Abu Dhabi or one of the corporate social tools like Yammer or Slack to enable collaboration, the idea of one-to-many and many-to-many communication is now the norm—mobile is the device of choice. Our mobile devices provide great efficiency and connectivity, enhancing our communication and ability to influence one another. Obviously, fourth revolution leaders will need to embrace every aspect of the enhancement that mobile devices allow.

MIND SWITCH FACT

According to Pew Research Center (April 1, 2015), here is how people use their mobile devices:

97 percent use text messaging

92 percent make voice calls

57 percent do online banking

55 percent get news

41 percent listen to music

30 percent take a class

18 percent submit job applications online

And keep in mind—such technology is not just for connecting with your team, potential clients, customers, and colleagues. You can also learn a great deal of information about other companies, competitors or otherwise, with a little bit of online digging and stay on top of new leadership trends.

Even with the greatest technological innovations or newfangled gadgets, however, leaders need to maintain the core principles that led to their success. A strong character, pride in doing your best, clarity, and depth won't come from a smartphone alone. You need to step up and confidently take the lead. You must be willing to empower your employees, recognize their accomplishments, and help them achieve their goals. Set the direction and tone for your team and

> "At the very least, if you are keeping up with developments and trying new things you are going to relate more easily to a diverse team in a workplace. You are also going to be more effective because you will use your ability to connect on a human level when it is most needed and use technology for everything else."

provide constructive feedback when necessary. Otherwise, technological advancement is all for naught.

> ### MIND SWITCH FACT
>
> Consider the "now everywhere" technology of touch screens. They date back to the 1960s when E. A. Johnson invented the system as a radar screen used by air traffic control. The technology was bulky, slow, imprecise, and very expensive and did not appear on consumer gadgets until the 1980s along with ATMs and checkout devices. It took Steve Jobs's leadership to change everything in 2007 with the iPhone. Touch screens are now everywhere in our homes and we love them.

It's Up to You

As with all technological development, there will be lovers and haters. There will be pros and cons. You must make choices every day to either embrace or resist the changes that technology facilitates. Wherever you lie on the spectrum from luddite (opposer of new technologies) to technophile (lover of new technologies), being curious and open-minded to the use of new technologies will be key to becoming a good fourth revolution leader. Keep in mind, there is an irrepressible human desire to innovate, so continuous change is inevitable. Innovation will bring a constant reassessment of how businesses operate and how leaders need to steer their teams. Good leaders will leverage all of these opportunities.

"Be happy, not scared by changes. Your attitude will largely affect your success."

《《〈〉》》

18

We urge you to make a mind switch: be the leader that stays relevant and inspires others by maintaining your curiosity about, and adopting, technologies that enhance the way we work. Whether talking about global connectivity or simply sharing a job posting with a colleague online, technology affects your every move. It has also led to an increasingly diverse workplace and the breakdown of what we call the workforce generation gap.

> **"Leaders need to think about tech tools available to them like the waves on a beach, they can either bring you onto the shore or pound you into the sand."**

MIND SWITCH FACT

Before the Internet generation almost every home in the United States had a landline phone; now over 40 percent of homes don't, according to researchers at the National Center for Health Statistics (July 2014). The youngest generation in the workforce doesn't even know what a landline is.

Demographics

The truth is that technology erases the "generation gap." Despite how old you are, utilizing new technologies can help you feel, act, and essentially be young again. An 84-year-old engineer who helped put the first man on the moon told us this: "Hell, I may get a lot younger next year with all that I'm learning online." On the flip side, however, technology can also exacerbate generation gaps—which is why great leaders must acknowledge and embrace differences and similarities in various age groups, including their own particular cultures and quirks, within the workforce.

You will soon find (if you haven't already) that your boss is a lot younger than you, your new hire wants to telecommute, and your hiring strategy includes a large freelance component. This is true for even the largest of companies that use platforms like Catalant Technologies to power their business talent needs in a flexible way. This era is both exciting and daunting as we think about what it means for how we need to work, how we manage our effectiveness as leaders, and how we grow organizations.

> "As much as things are different, one thing remains the same: every generation looks at the one that follows them as the generation that will take down society. They haven't yet."

Differences in the mix of generations in the new world of work will sometimes lead to tension as people interpret rules through their own lenses. Only in the military will you find unity where people both know, and are required to follow, the same rules. In the armed services, members are similar in the way they dress and act and are generally the same age, carry the same tools or weapons, and face punishment if they don't do what they are told.

None of that is true in the workforce in general.

It is important to note that this isn't a new phenomenon. The workforce has never been a totally unified group. For example, the first industrial revolution had a melting pot of immigrants who laid the path for the "greatest generation"—the only uniting factor was the need to survive.

Aside from age differences, contrasts in cultural, ethnic, religious, and racial backgrounds can be found everywhere. For example, there are higher percentages of people from different countries and cultures in our workforce today. Not everyone speaks or understands a single language at the same level, and people don't necessarily dress or think alike. The workforce, like the modern family, is becoming increasingly blended.

The Generation Breakdown

As a leader, you need to have a strong familiarity with the different generational groups that you are likely to encounter throughout your career—including the traits that characterize them. It's important to note that different sources cite the ages in each of these demographic groups similarly, but they may vary by one or two years. Also, the "defining characteristics" of each group are not black and white, but grey. It's important to acknowledge the reality that you get labeled as one generation or another solely based on the year you were born. You could have been born at the tail end or at the start of any grouped age and have a hybrid of defining characteristics, some of which entirely defy your typical generation member.

THE "GREATEST GENERATION"

People born between 1901 and 1945 are part of what Tom Brokaw labeled the "greatest generation." They are sometimes called the Silent Generation, G.I. Generation, or Depression Cohort. Their defining characteristics are having a sense of purpose and duty to country (shaped by WWII) as well as working extremely hard to better themselves.

BABY BOOMERS

People born between 1946 and 1964 are referred to as baby boomers, the Boom Generation, or, in the subculture, Hippies.

Their defining characteristics tend toward freedom and experimentation, but they still hold work in high value. They saw the assassination of President John F. Kennedy and Nixon's Watergate (which led to disillusionment and distrust of the government) and were the first to see a man on the moon.

This generation's retirement rate is a leading factor in the transformation of the workforce. Roughly 10,000 boomers will be leaving the workforce every day over a 19-year period according to Pew Research Center. (Some of you may be grimacing and some of you may be cheering about this shift.) Though a portion of baby boomers have adapted, as a generalization they are not nearly as involved with, or enthralled by, technology as younger generations. Their exit will therefore bring dramatic changes in the way that the workforce interacts with each other and the way that leaders will need to think about their utilization of technology and media.

GEN X
People born between 1965 and 1980 are referred to as Gen X, Baby Busters, and the MTV Generation. They experienced a series of recessions, the AIDS epidemic, and the end of the Cold War. Their defining characteristic is being the first generation to embrace the Internet. They value autonomy and freedom at their jobs, and they are less work-centric than older generations. They are considered to be motivated by compensation and career potential, while being relatively less concerned with social causes. The mobile phone and e-mail are their communication tools of choice.

MILLENNIALS
People born between 1981 and 2003 are referred to as Net Gen, Nexters, Echo Boomer, GenNext, Boomerang

Generation, Peter Pan Generation, or most commonly, Millennials. Their defining characteristics are valuing work but expecting quick advancement and having little loyalty to any one organization for very long. They use their smartphones frequently (aided by advancing technology), have big student debts, and live at home longer.

By 2020, the Y or Millennial generation will make up around 50 percent of the workforce. The four strongest characteristics of this generation are that they accept speed as a reality, care about the world more, are used to communicating in a variety of ways, and are willing to embrace technologies that help them do so. These traits alone bode very well for the next leadership wave and give us reasons to rail against the trend of "millennial-trashing."

They enjoy a relatively seamless mashup of work and personal life as they feel their job should contribute to the greater good. Social media websites are their communication tools of choice.

GEN Z

People born after 2003, the post-millennial generation, are loosely called Gen Z or iGen. This generation, which has not yet entered the work force en masse, is global, social, visual, and technologically advanced. According to Pew Research (April 2016), their 69 million members in the United States will soon outnumber the millennials before them.

They value practical career choices but are susceptible to distractions in all aspects of their lives. They are considered less developed in face-to-face social interaction and conflict resolution skills, but highly developed in online collaboration. The tablet, smartphone, and visual social media sites are their tools of choice. Having grown up with smartphones

> **"Be very nice to the next generation because you're probably going to work for them someday."**

and the Internet, they are extremely tech savvy. They also exhibit shorter attention spans and a drive for immediate gratification, causing them to focus on speed, whether in communication or services. According to Mintel Research, 60 percent have used only emojis to communicate at times.

According to the federal government's "Youth Risk Behavior Surveillance Survey," which surveyed 10,000 high school students, Gen Z is also shaping up to be the best-behaved generation ever. Only 15 percent of today's teens smoke compared to 30.5 percent 20 years ago. They also binge drink less, use drugs less, carry fewer weapons, and watch less television than all previous generations.

MIND SWITCH FACT

90 percent of millennials are social media users.
76 percent of Gen X are social media users.
59 percent of boomers are social media users.

Source: eMarketer

Leading Across the Generations

So how do these generational differences affect the way you lead? The primary contrasts relate to the way leaders:

- » **Learn** (need to be insatiably curious to become enlightened)
- » **Communicate** (need to use a wider set of tools, with technology being key)

>> **Inspire** (need to empower people by helping them remove their personal barriers to progress)

You need to understand the generational differences between groups so you can work with your colleagues and employees more efficiently and effectively. For example, younger generations seem to want more freedom in the way they do their work, but they also want more mentoring from their bosses. They don't want to stay in jobs as long as their parents did, and they seem to prefer collaboration over competition. The boomers (who wield a lot of power as the majority of the "higher-ups") value a structure of command and control in the workforce to some degree—a leadership style that is becoming unrealistic today.

The negative "dog eat dog" and "survival of the fittest" environment that boomers had to accept is vanishing. Teams today want to be empowered to do a great job and to work *together* for a leader who inspires them toward new and bold things. If they don't get this experience, they will likely move on to their own venture, the start-up next door, or a more progressive company.

> "The younger person asks, 'Why should I do that?' 'What's in it for me?' or says, 'I don't want to.'"

Today, research shows that younger generations plan to stay in their jobs for a shorter length of time. Turnover is costly ($15,000 to $25,000 according to a *Forbes,* Feb. 2016 Huffington Post blog by Julie Kanor), and any time employees are inspired by the example a leader sets, they are encouraged to stay longer. This means the reverse is also true: investing in your up-and-coming team may be a risky bet because they might be gone before you are able to reap the rewards.

Deloitte found in its Global Millennials Survey (2017) that two-thirds of millennials said they hoped to be working for a different organization in five years or sooner. One in four would quit immediately if they had another offer. And nearly half said they would quit within two years regardless. The reasons behind these stats are plentiful: some attribute this attitude to peer pressure or the desire to be a "mover and shaker" in an industry. Another reason is simply that some are making poor choices or decisions, not knowing themselves or their strengths early enough in their careers. Finally, some millennials just want to experiment and try something new.

With the high cost of recruitment, and potentially poor retention rates, companies are increasingly seeing the need to invest in their leadership talent because a good leader might make a difference in workers' decisions to stay or go. As we've stated, people work for *leaders*, not companies.

MIND SWITCH FACT

An average Gen X or Y worker will send 20 texts a day, whereas the 41 percent of older workers don't send even one.

Pew Research Center, Sept. 2016 Text Message Survey

Our Similarities

In addition to the mixed generations, there are a wide variety of ethnicities, cultures, traditions, religions, geography, education, experiences, priorities, personal preferences, and levels of tech savviness in today's workforce. While diversity brings with it some complexity, there are more similarities than dissimilarities when you take a broad view across all ages, races, or creeds. You can choose any two people sitting around you right now, and regardless of their backgrounds, ages, or heritage, they may be equally as likely to:

> "Amateurs deal well with people like themselves. Pros deal well with people who aren't like themselves."

» Like three-day weekends
» Prefer home-grown tomatoes over store-bought
» Like kitten and puppy videos
» Enjoy a sunny day over a rainy one
» Want to have food on the table and a roof over their head
» Want their family to be healthy and untroubled
» Think their children are the smartest in the class
» Want to have satisfying work
» Want to be happy
» Want to be appreciated
» Believe in life on other planets
» Derail because of alcohol, marijuana, or mad love

And that list will be true for people in Sudan and Switzerland, as well as San Francisco or Seattle.

The Mind Switch on Leading Today and Tomorrow

Today's business world needs leaders willing to evolve with the rapidly changing workplace. Whether considering new technologies that are connecting the global workforce in ways we never imagined, or shifting demographics influencing business cultures, leaders need to be open to new information, experiences, ideas, and opinions. Technology cannot replace the set values of transparency, strong communication, confidence, and hard work, but it does affect how these values are expressed. It is also a major tool for any leader—simply put; you have to move with the times. The same goes for working with a multigenerational team: you can't be stodgy and stuck in your ways. Flexibility is imperative, as is the ability to consider others' viewpoints and be sensitive toward everyone's differences—even if you're not quite sure what emoji to use at first.

STORIES FROM THE ROAD

Bob Berkowitz, who has a global personal and corporate communications practice specializing in media, presentation, and sales training (www.bobberkowitz.com), writes about communicating across generations.

Few things have revolutionized the way we communicate more than social media. Your idea in Columbus, Ohio, can be spread around the world in minutes. Influence is infinite.

And yet, at some point, no matter how connected you are digitally, you're going to have to look someone in the eye and make your case. That has not changed. No one is going to give you millions of dollars to invest in your business via a 140-character tweet. They'll expect you to lay out your vision and plans for a business idea that needs funding. You can expect to be asked penetrating questions. This kind of in-person presentation—be it for a start-up, someone looking for a job, speaking to the media, the board of directors, or employees—does not come easily or naturally for most people. Especially for the rising generations that rely heavily on devices for their communication. So what to do?

1. Have a clear purpose and idea of what you want to say.
2. Be "them" oriented—that is, understand the people you are speaking to. Who are they? What do they want? What are their dreams and aspirations? Fears and anxieties? How do your ideas benefit them? You also need to answer their unasked question: Why should they care? When you understand life from their point of view, then you can tailor your messages to meet their expectations.
3. Tell stories. Lots of them. Stories create a visual picture of what you are talking about. They bring your presentation to life. And as an added bonus, stories are memorable. They stick to the brain. Data? Not so much.
4. Feelings count. We make the vast majority of our decisions based more on how we feel about something and not what we think about. Find the emotional reason why someone will be interested in what you are talking about.
5. Here's what's possible. If they take the actions you want, how will their lives be better?

RETHINKING OUR LEADERSHIP QUALITIES

02

L eadership is ever evolving—it isn't an act, it's a lifestyle. Real leaders don't just think about leadership all the time, they live it day in and day out until it becomes second nature. Although leading others is not rocket science, it's also not something you can learn in a three-day off-site. Being a successful leader takes constant, subtle pressure to get better and more effective over time. In the current era of lightning speed changes and 24/7 connectivity; self-discipline and willingness to learn is needed more than ever to become and stay a relevant leader. Regardless of the current disrupted workplace, some things haven't changed: a leader has to set a course and develop a team that collaborates, cooperates, and (hopefully) enjoys each other.

During our years of coaching and working with executives, we've been fortunate enough to meet many amazing leaders who have given us inspiration and many lessons on how they became who they are today. They have ranged from fortune 100 CEOs to chief financial officers, chief technology officers, chief procurement officers, chief digital officers, chief marketing officers, business luminaries, line managers, heads of supply chain, brand leaders, divisional presidents, founders of disruptive companies, and entrepreneurs.

> **"Your leaders want you to lead. Your people want to be led."**

Through observing these outstanding leaders, we learned that they generally tend to be more:

» Personally accountable
» Informed and curious about the wider world
» Committed to both their job and the job of the whole organization
» Emotionally stable
» Positive in a negative situation

They also have:

» A combo of competencies, traits, experiences, roles, personality inclinations, and values that fits the needs of their organization
» An understanding that they must maintain morale, engage stakeholders, and remain trusted
» The ability to get a group of high-powered individuals to cooperatively interact with one mind, one heart, and one voice

» A willingness to engage

» A comfort with ambiguity

» An ethno-cultural empathy

» The capability to easily relate across generations

» Cognitive flexibility and openness

» Varied interests beyond the office

» Willingness to show their true self when the environment allows for it

» Solid relationships with their work partners, especially their executive assistants

» A mindset where success is considered a derivative of not only their own efforts, but also the efforts of those around them

In researching *The Leadership Mind Switch*, we also wanted to learn from the "up and comers." We asked many Gen X and Y rising leaders what they *want* in a leader and found out that while some leadership qualities will never change, others must.

To be successful in such an environment, it's truly a matter of rethinking the qualities and behaviors that contribute to stellar leadership. You need to understand not only the new attitudes and actions that are worth developing, but also those that are time-tested and evergreen. In this chapter, we'll look at four major qualities in regards to leadership attitudes that are imperative for today's leaders. (In Chapter 3, we'll extend the discussion to the behaviors that today's leaders must exhibit.) The first quality is one that gets a lot of lip service, but also seems to fall by the wayside in the bustle of the fourth industrial revolution: trust.

True Blue: Stay Trustworthy Beyond Reproach

In our survey of over 500 emerging leaders, we asked what three words best typify the qualities of ideal leadership. The top responses were all variations of the words "trust," "trusted," and "trustworthy." As we further discussed this topic, we decided that the term "true blue" best describes this trait. "True blue" resonates deeply with us as we see it as a step beyond "being trusted"—it also includes the idea of authenticity and transparency. Historically, the expression "true blue" goes back to the medieval period in a time when all colors were given symbolic significance; blue was the symbol of loyalty, constancy, faithfulness, and truth. It is also a very common Australian slang term meaning loyal and trustworthy.

> **"The West Point Cadet Honor Code reads simply: 'A cadet will not lie, cheat, or steal, or tolerate those who do.' Works in business, too."**

As a leader, the quality of trustworthiness, or being true blue, is the area in which you want to receive the highest rating in performance reviews. Without trust, nothing else you do matters: your good work, your creativity, your brilliance will always be suspect. Colleagues, coworkers, employees, and bosses must have a firm belief in your reliability and honesty—you should expect the same from those around you. Exhibiting such qualities will also help those people you lead develop similar attitudes.

Whether in person or online, trust works two ways:

1. You need to *be* trusted so people will choose to follow you.

2. You need to *be able* to trust people you choose to work with.

When trustworthy leaders decide on something, they make it very clear that they will do what they say. They keep their word. This makes them reliable. If people can count on you to follow through on your stated plans or actions, then you'll be viewed as trustworthy. If you exhibit your trustworthiness at all times—in front of others, online, and even behind closed doors—people will follow you. You also must instill trust with the individual members of your team consistently.

One aspect of developing a trusting relationship is maintaining a sense of openness and transparency with the people you work with. You must be accessible and willing to have frank, honest discussions.

Being true blue, however, doesn't mean you have to say everything that is on your mind or everything you plan to do at all times, but it does mean you don't distort or play loose with the facts. Staying tight-lipped on certain matters or playing a situation close to the vest is entirely fair behavior—you're not being untrustworthy, simply discreet. While you're thinking through a problem or a plan, you don't need to discuss every detail with your team—not only would that be time-consuming, but some information may be sensitive and necessary to keep quiet for the time being. Truthfulness does not mean divulgence.

> **"As a leader, to be trusted and trustworthy, do what you say you will do when you say you will do it. Simply telling no lies beats having talent any day."**

MIND SWITCH FACT

A 2015 Pew Research Center report (*Millennials in Adulthood*) showed:

» 19 percent of millennials say "most people can't be trusted."
» 31 percent of Gen Xers say "most people can't be trusted."
» 80 percent of boomers say "most people can't be trusted."

This data perspective on trust shows boomers as pessimistic cynics. This is not surprising to us because they've been around a long time and have had many work and personal experiences, both good and bad. They have seen people in positions of authority and power behave inconsistently, change their stance or opinion at will, renege on their decisions, put on a show displaying confidence or knowledge they didn't have, and broken rules and lied.

Truth Depends on Your Lens

One of the features of a global and technology-fueled workforce is that trustworthiness is viewed in many different ways by different groups of people—it's all in the eye of the beholder. You need to be able to trust others, and be trusted by them, no matter their culture, age, socioeconomic status, gender, first language, or religious affiliations. Truth, however, is viewed through the lens of a person's cultural and geographic upbringing. There is no "universal truth" because we are working in a world of countless cultures. Your customers and employees around the world will most likely think differently from you. Deeply rooted perspectives on integrity, transparency, and even honesty may differ between these cultures.

For example, you may be managing operations in a different country or, at the very least, have staff in countries other than the United States. We authors, along with many U.S.-based companies, do business in India, the Middle East, Indonesia, South Africa, Sweden, China, Switzerland, Germany, the United Kingdom, and Spain. In such a multinational workforce, you cannot simply impose your *personal* definitions of corporate integrity on policy and practices. They need to be clearly stated and agreed upon, especially in tough areas like anticorruption and bribery, two systemic problems in many businesses in developing nations (not to mention in the United States). Developing and keeping clear policies will build trust among your staff and business partners, no matter where they are located.

In some countries, your customers or colleagues from the region will say, due to their culture, "Yes, I can do that," knowing fully that they cannot and will not be able to perform a certain task or service. The lack of transparency from, say, an American point of view, fosters *dis*trust and can only lead to problems down the line. It's difficult, however, since in such a situation, some groups of people wouldn't see this promise as lying (according to their own cultural norms), even though they know there's no way they'll be able to keep their word. One media VP told me about her young manager who agreed to meet a time deadline, then missed it by a day. He was eager to explain why this happened: "But I worked a day longer on it." In his mind, missing the agreed-upon deadline was acceptable because he actually worked longer. Most U.S. businesses would *not* see this response as a valid

> **"Understand what they mean versus what you mean."**

excuse. In his cultural norms, however, it was a fine remedy to the situation.

In some Germanic cultures it's just as serious to break "process" as it is to break the rules—meaning the failure to follow an established process is seen as untrustworthy as if you actually lied, stole, or cheated. The definition of appropriate behavior varies from country to country, culture to culture, and sometimes from season to season.

You therefore need to ensure that people understand what "trust" means under your leadership, whether at home or abroad. Outline the particulars—those specific values and qualities that you believe contribute to a trustworthy business environment and relationship. You must be so simple and clear in your explanation that anyone can understand what you need and expect. However, you don't want to provide so many messages that people become muddled or lose track and fail to comprehend them. Anywhere from three to five strong messages should be easiest for people to understand. For example, messages could include:

» Any customer interaction is a representation of the organization, you must be willing to share any and all details of correspondence, meetings, and other interactions. This is the only way we can all protect and grow the business.
» We expect that you will be consistent in your work. You will come every day, be available for others, and say what you mean to your colleagues. This will make for a more trusted environment where we can thrive.

Make sure to repeat, localize, and personalize these messages as necessary so there is no grey area.

You're Only Human

Even with the best intentions, as a leader you can still slip up when it comes to the values we're discussing. You may forget something you committed to, tell a story incorrectly based on how you remember it, or someone may simply misinterpret something you said or did that can appear to be a mistruth. This is called being human.

Leaders are not expected to be superhuman, in fact the idea of true blue being "the real thing" means that you are who you are. Trustworthiness can be sustained if you are steadfast in clearing the air when you do slip up with something you've said, done, or implied. The key to being a good leader in such situations is to approach and remedy them privately (so that means on the phone or in person, not in an e-mail or text) and ask for clarification. Explain or apologize, whichever is necessary, and try to learn from the misstep. This also applies in reverse: trusting those around you is equally important as being trusted, so let go of mistakes if the intent was pure.

> **"One of the worst things you can do as a leader is to be unforgiving of a mistake and hang onto it for years."**

Kindly Confident: Project and Inspire Confidence

It is no longer the norm or the aspiration for people to work for someone in a position of power who simply directs without context. In addition to building trust, leaders must also project confidence and help others develop this quality. Confidence is a combination of courage and curiosity. Courage is taking necessary action, despite your fears. Curiosity is your desire to continuously learn about new concepts and ideas, and it acts as a driver toward success. Combining these two traits creates an unstoppable and confident leader.

> "Confidence in a leader is as much to instill it in others as oneself. Having confidence isn't knowing things will work out; it's knowing you can work with whatever happens."

Confident people make a realistic assessment of their accomplishments, skills, and strengths so they know who they are and who they aren't, understand their limitations, and can work on their weaknesses. They listen to their inner voice and don't frivolously seek approval from others—they don't need constant reassurance, but they know when to ask for help. Such a mindset contributes to the respect they are given by colleagues, bosses, managers, and employees.

"Kindly" confident people are those who are not only confident, but also positive and optimistic, allowing them to assume the best in their team. They are generous rather than judgmental or cocky. Curt Carter, CEO of America, Inc., and Debra's favorite mentor, sums the "kindly confident" concept like this: "If 30 people are on a desert island the most confident member of the group will become the leader—if he [or she] is absent of bravado."

Being kindly confident speaks to the need to master your fears of the new and the unknown with an authenticity and vulnerability that used to seem "fluffy" in the workplace. In the past, confidence used to be recognized by the image of strength and directive communication styles, a willingness to make bold assertions, and the ability to take the hill with force. We believe the twist that is needed for the fourth industrial revolution is based on an attitude that is somewhat more humble and caring, yet no less impactful.

Kindly confident leaders are generous with their teams and take the time to truly get to know their people. In doing so, many leaders find that their team members are just as smart as they are, maybe got better grades, often have superior electronic savvy, and have a wide array of interesting heritages and cultural backgrounds. In a diverse demographic environment, being humble and caring will open conversations and potential opportunities to connect, influence, and lead that wouldn't happen otherwise. The old way of assuming that leadership meant being the "head honcho" or the "chosen one" just won't fly anymore.

> **"Everyone has times of insecurity. Leaders don't let it show."**

Optimistically Inspire Others

Universally, people welcome energetic and positive vibes in any situation, but for leaders, these vibes are necessary for survival. You must see the upside in different situations and energize those around you. You should be positive and optimistic in all situations, which will display confidence in yourself and in your team's abilities. You still need to be fully aware of potential risks and your responsibilities, but keeping that positive attitude will be contagious to those you lead. Your team will live what they learn from you.

A good attitude goes a long way in projecting, and inspiring, confidence. Today, a good attitude is "not having an attitude." This means not harboring convictions or opinions that are judgmental or critical in nature. You must be careful with how you develop, explain, and vocalize your thoughts. You'll find that your mindset and attitudes change when you alter your perception of a situation. Set an example for those around you by managing your perspective in a constructive and productive way. You need to empower your team to meet and exceed expectations and overcome challenges.

Still, even the greatest, most optimistic attitude will not save you from every roadblock or problem that is likely to occur. Being confident also means being realistic when you need to be. Look for and expect the best, but plan for the worst. And if it ends up being the worst, be tenacious and have the confidence to try again.

Tempering Your Confidence

As mentioned, no one wants to work for an overconfident, egotistical boss—keep this in mind in any leadership position. The days of the "big dogs" running the show are over. Leaders are not infallible, nor should they pretend to be. In fact, the ability to adapt, modify, and potentially revise a plan after you've made a decision sets a positive example for followers as much as having made the right decision in the first place. Just as with the concept of trust: we're all human, we make mistakes, and we certainly don't know everything!

Leaders need to be confident in their staff's capabilities and willing to hear them out. There is so much we can learn from each other. Kindly confident leaders understand that other people's opinions, attributes, and knowledge may surpass their own, and they must have the courage to recognize and embrace this fact. Leaders must have the confidence to ask about what they don't know or request help in unfamiliar areas. It takes a comfort in your own skin, and a sureness of self, to share

> "An executive's secret hell is being in over your head ... and it's more of the time than we let on."

the spotlight with others. You need to merge your knowledge and your team's together, recognizing that you don't need to be the only one to come up with new ideas, projects, or initiatives.

Technology advancements are an area where we regularly see a lack of confidence in more experienced leaders. Not only on a basic functional level, but at a higher and less tangible one: leaders today must "dream big," because if they don't, technology will surpass them. Dreaming big takes courage because today's technological advances are huge. Regardless of a leader's generation, you now need to lean toward early adoption of new technological changes. It takes confidence and optimism to "gamble" on new products, services, methods of communication, and more, but it also takes an equal amount of confidence to ask for help when necessary.

Lastly, confidence doesn't mean you aren't scared sometimes. Just like the rest of us, even the best leaders sweat everywhere—hands, armpits, behind their knees—when they think of the

> **"I'm terrified, but I do it just to see if I can get through it."**

potential ramifications of any single decision. One executive told us, "The roots of my hair are scared." They push on though because they care about their people and their customers, the environment and social changes, and making a difference in the world. Of course making money and keeping shareholders happy is important, too, but the idea of "caring" truly leads to newfound confidence and ultimate success.

As Mark Zuckerberg has said, in his open letter on Facebook's tenth anniversary in 2014, about why his partners and he were the ones to build Facebook: "we just cared more."

Enlightened: Open Your Mind and Constantly Learn

Just as with the quality of confidence, curiosity plays a major role in maintaining a sense of "enlightenment." Here, we're not referring to spiritual enlightenment, but to a leader's ability to stay well informed and to approach every interaction free of prejudices or ignorance. An effective leader is intellectually curious, constantly learning, interested in things beyond the obvious, and genuinely in pursuit of wisdom about people, places, technologies, religions, scientific advances, economies, and cultures. This list of interests seems to set a very high bar, but being enlightened is only limited by your willingness to "know what you don't know" and to soak in new information without the biases that often inhibit learning.

Most of us put effort into learning what is familiar and pertains directly to ourselves. The best (and often most innovative) leaders, however, take an interest in a wide range of ideas, topics, problems, and solutions. Enlightened leaders are intellectually curious by nature. In order to energize and empower their teams, they take an earnest, serious path of perpetual exploration and experimentation, trying new and at least different approaches. They listen to what customers, employees, competitors, friends, the market, and society want and need, and they adapt their plans to be able to deliver. They know that every problem they face is an opportunity to learn, and every time they fail to learn, the problem will reoccur.

> **"Every single day, every single hour I ask myself, 'Why don't I know that?,' then I tell myself I never was exposed to it. I never learned it. I forgot it. But then I remedy it."**

Continuously Learning

Enlightened leaders learn something new every day utilizing a myriad of channels about their industry, business, work, and outside interests so they can try to create something new the following day. They are results-oriented problem solvers that seek information to become better. They constantly broaden their knowledge through researching topics or trends they've never been exposed to, never learned about, or have simply forgotten. They don't bring baggage to conversations based on how they were raised, the religion they belong to, or their politics. All of these factors shape who they are but shouldn't get in the way of understanding other people and their ideas.

"Do be prepared, but don't be scared."

Enlightened leaders have a great attitude supplemented by the habit of continually reading, talking, seeking, listening, and observing. They are open-minded in their pursuit of knowledge and are nonjudgmental about where it comes from. Leaders must think objectively, laterally, and independently. They must also be willing to question concepts, ideas, and even facts in today's information-saturated society.

Enlightenment can come from so many sources—your choices now are endless. Technology has made the pursuit of enlightenment easier than ever. You can delve into blogs and websites, online digital archives, Instagram feeds, Twitter, Quora, and more. The world—past, present, and future—is literally at your fingertips. The problem is, it's at everyone else's, too, making it difficult to keep a competitive advantage. Information that used to be reserved for "the top" is available to every person in the free world. More worrisome is that there is so much to sort through to find what's important, relevant, and necessary.

In times of digital deluge, sometimes it's best to go "old school." For example, Bill Gates read 50 books last year. It can also be helpful to read material or get information from alternative outlets including ones you wouldn't typically consult. Doing so will provide you with new perspectives, a way to connect with people different than you, and interesting tidbits to open a conversation that could become exceptional. Some of the greatest resources for continuous learning, however, are your staff, colleagues, and partners.

Enlightenment and critical thinking go hand in hand with asking questions, and the skill of asking questions is truly in listening to the answers. Enlightened leaders ask intentional questions and listen closely to the responses in order to make high quality decisions. They use those answers to produce results through business and team relationships.

Effective leaders are known more by the questions they ask then the answers they give. They ask questions that are challenging enough to be useful but not so harsh as to seem hostile, interrogatory, or debilitating. They ask what's important: what needs to change in a project or work environment and what needs to remain the same.

> **"Questions minimize mutual misunderstanding and miscommunication, and they cause people to respond because questions are an active exchange. Plus, questions let you in on the juicy stuff in life."**

In the words of Steve Jobs, former CEO of Apple, "It doesn't make sense to hire smart people and tell them what to do; we hire smart people so they can tell us what to do." Every person has something to tell you or teach you; with multiculturalism and rapid technological change this reality is magnified. An enlightened leader knows this and seeks out perspectives from every corner. You must ask the right questions and exhibit attentiveness during the responses. Without this skill, you won't get commitment or consensus from your team, those people that you need to be on board with your actions, plans, and steps toward success.

> "Good leaders ask lots of questions, but they also question themselves, their decisions, their approach, and their impact."

Imparting Knowledge

With the constant changes of this era, there is no documentation on how to proceed in many aspects of our working world. There often isn't enough time or ability to hold lengthy meetings and arrive at a consensus, nor is there reporting of past precedents to guide you. Instead, you have to use your critical thinking skills and acquired business acumen to come up with a solution and move forward. As an enlightened leader, you have to help others around you gain the necessary knowledge to succeed, not only for their individual sake, but also for the sake of the organization as a whole.

By way of example, high-potential but relatively unseasoned team members often want immediate changes in processes and policy. If management doesn't hop to it and meet their demands, these team members may become demoralized, which can grow into contempt for management. What the unseasoned don't always think about, know, or grasp is the complexity of many situations—company financials and regulatory obligations need to be taken into account, along with a company's position in an industry, goals, overall strategies, and extended history.

As leaders, we have to provide these team members with context, help them to think critically and to explore the global implications before making decisions. It is important for rising leaders to understand that information doesn't immediately lead to critical thinking and ultimately good decision making. In fact, Nathaniel Carr, a cognitive psychologist, says the Internet encourages an *uncritical* kind of thinking, meaning that many people today simply accept constructed nonsensical statements as profound, particularly on the Internet (*The Shallows: What the Internet Is Doing to Our Brains*, 2008, W. W. Norton & Co.). Lots of information doesn't necessarily lead to knowledge—it is how we use that information wisely that causes us to learn and grow.

Since that's the case, your goal as a leader is to impart knowledge not readily available on the Internet or even in a book. That's where your character, communication, and spirit of developing the members of your team will separate you from other leaders. It is where your problem-solving skills come into play to match information with logic, open-mindedness, fairness, and the use of abstract ideas to come up with rational solutions to problems.

> **"Complaining about a problem without posing a solution is really just whining."**

Tenacious: Be Persistent in Your Pursuits

All the qualities discussed so far in this chapter—trust, confidence, and enlightenment—are imperative for today's leaders. But without persistence and grit, the other three attributes will fail to materialize. True leaders must be tenacious, determined, and self-starting. They can take a tough situation and fix it or make it better. They might retrench, reiterate, reconvene, or pivot more often than other leaders, but they keep at it instead of stalling when something becomes difficult. Even when they don't succeed, they don't quit. Remember: nothing significant happens with little effort.

Over the years, there has been much written about "grit," which is very similar to tenacity—but we prefer the language of "tenacity" because of the visual image it produces when used in relation to hard things like metal or wood. It implies hardiness and moxie all at once. For us, it encompasses both grit and persistence.

Our favorite speaker and author on the topic of grit is Angela Duckworth, an American psychologist who has studied grit for more than a decade and has even built a tool to measure it. Without downplaying the depth of her analysis, the extreme CliffsNotes version of her findings is that grit is a predictor of achievement and is not yoked to IQ, meaning it is a quality that we can all develop. Her 2007 groundbreaking study, *Grit: Perserverance and Passion for Long-Term Goals*, (which was published in the *Journal of Personality and Social Psychology*), defined grit as:

> perseverance and passion for long-term goals. Grit entails working strenuously toward challenges, maintaining effort and interest over years despite failure, adversity, and plateaus in progress. The gritty individual approaches achievement as a marathon; his or her advantage is stamina. Whereas disappointment or boredom signals to others that it is time to change trajectory and cut losses, the gritty individual stays the course.

Note the words and phrases Duckworth uses to describe grit: "working strenuously," "maintaining effort," "stamina," "staying the course." Not only is she referring to follow-through, but also follow-up. As a resolute leader, when you try something and it doesn't work, you must try again. Approach the problem in a slightly different way and repeat. It takes mental and physical discipline, especially in the face of failure, but fortitude will help you overcome even the most difficult obstacles.

Tenacious leaders are not only gritty, they are also usually self-starting—they initiate instead of waiting. When you are the one to start something new, say a project or program, you are the one applying the pressure, not feeling it. Leaders don't wait until the heavens open and the angels sing to start—they are working constantly toward their goals. Persistence and grit helps them push through barriers.

> "Like honesty trumps talent, grit usually does too."

In It for the Long Haul

There are many professions and pursuits where being tenacious is clearly a behavior that differentiates winners from the rest—think about long-distance athletes, astronauts, Mt. Everest climbers, brain surgeons, or Navy Seals. But in broader business and government leadership, the idea of tenacity is often overlooked in favor of more visible and sometimes superficial qualities like "charisma."

This tendency is short-sighted: it takes time and mastery to impact the world in any meaningful sense. Recall Duckworth's definition of grit: it includes "perseverance and passion for *long-term* goals." Sweeping, positive change is often only recognized long after the leader who initiated it has gone. The ability to realize your vision and see it through is a quality of a true leader. How much time it takes doesn't matter—only the quality of the outcome.

50

Still, it is easy to get derailed, especially with disruptions around every corner. Globalization has made the playing field not only flatter but also wider. Technological advancements have decreased the barriers to entering new industries and, in turn, accelerated the ability for people from all over the world to emerge as new competitors.

With so many options, directions, and distractions, it is easy to get derailed. Consistent persistence, however, will get you further faster. Your strength of character and will and your commitment to staying the course over time send a positive, unifying message to your team. People follow resolve, and a leader's tenacity builds trust, empowers others, and communicates a strong leadership example, but you have to be willing to stick with it.

For example, a great deal of persistence—time and lawyer fees—went into Airbnb founder Brian Chesky's fight with New York City Council members. The council had introduced a bill that would fine Airbnb hosts up to $50,000 each for renting their apartments. The battle for Airbnb in marquis cities around the world is likely to last for years. Less tenacious leaders than Brian Chesky might have bent under the weight of regulated industry titans and regulators themselves trying to push them out of their markets. As we wrote this book Airbnb was faced with another hurdle where users could be fined in the thousands.

> "Do take every minute as a chance to do something; more than others and better . . . put an all-out effort to avoid being viciously mediocre."

Be Gritty, Not Stubborn

We want to make sure that in all of this talk about "grit," you also understand that we're not simply saying "stick to your guns at all costs, even when you're wrong." Tenacity is not stubbornness. One manager we spoke to described another particularly stubborn one as "a ruthless jerk on the way to hell." That's not what we want for you, and how to get team members to follow you!

Being tenacious does not mean being blind to reality. It means finding a way when you truly believe in the path you want to follow, while still being humble and self-aware enough to know when to change tactics or to make a decision to stop what you are doing. Chesky, for example, was turned down by five out of seven investors, and two never bothered to reply. And of course, he's not the only one to stick to his convictions.

People forget that Bill Gates's first company, Traf-O-Data, a business developed to create reports for roadway engineers from raw traffic data, flopped. Or that Oprah was fired from her first television job because they said she was "unfit for television." Steve Jobs was ousted from the company he founded during a boardroom coup later to return as CEO and develop the iPod, iPhone, and iPad. Failure isn't a predictor of future failures—the tenacious leader learns and moves on with the wisdom gained.

The Mind Switch on Rethinking Our Leadership Qualities

The four main qualities that leaders need to succeed in today's ever-changing business world are trust, confidence, enlightenment, and tenacity. If there is no trust, all is for naught. Trust works both ways: I trust you will do what you say you will, and you can trust me to do the same. Breaking trust erodes confidence in people and in the system they are working in. You need a personal self-confidence so that you can handle what comes your way, but you also need confidence in the system and your manager. That comes from trusting what was said and done. Incessantly seeking information to confirm, reinforce, and tie in with your commitments builds trust and confidence. But all those attributes are soft compared to the nose-to-the-grindstone grit to turn ideas, thoughts, dreams, and goals into undeterred action.

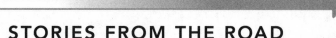

STORIES FROM THE ROAD

Christopher G. Lis, former president of Revolution Healthcare Partners LLC, writes about leading "across ages and functions."

Listen, learn, and appreciate: the keys to organizational transformation.

Years ago, I served on the senior leadership team of a health care organization that was pioneering the integration of traditional medical therapy with innovative complementary supportive care. We knew that this groundbreaking approach would make us a lightning rod for criticism and, therefore, we needed to transform our culture into one that was patient-centric, yet data driven, to demonstrate the wisdom of our approach.

I was asked to lead the company's transformation. At the time, I was a new non-physician executive in an organization dominated by seasoned clinicians, many of whom were resistant to change. At the same time, we employed many Gen Xer clinicians and non-clinicians who were open to change, yet seemed unmotivated.

My job was to clarify the power of our new strategy, define a process to integrate it into our operations, energize our multigenerational teams, and build companywide support to move to action.

Despite some uncertainty about how each individual would ultimately fit in, I was convinced the new strategy would drive unprecedented growth and create a platform for everyone to succeed—if only we could overcome the resistance. Yes, people had differing opinions, but we had common ground too: everyone was committed to doing better by our patients. My job was to inspire and engage, prove the success of our integrated strategy, and share our success stories.

First, I learned each team member's background, expectations, and opinions through in-person, phone, and e-mail discussions tailored to each generation. Equally importantly, I sought to understand how each individual viewed his or her role and wanted leadership to help advance their work in ways aligned with our strategy. I clarified what motivated and excited our teams, what they thought could be improved, and how their talents could best support our shared goals and objectives.

At first, some individuals were resistant, skeptical, or unmotivated. After weeks of conversations, however, shared interests emerged and our relationships moved toward mutual trust, understanding, and respect. The wisdom of the new strategy became clear and exciting to more and more people.

In addition, we recognized and rewarded the early adopters and innovators and showcased their contributions to senior leadership and the board of directors. We also tailored incentives toward individual preferences, whether financial rewards, time off, or public recognition. As a result, trust was built brick by brick as we built relationships, discerned motivations, and delivered on our promises.

As momentum increased, new treatments benefiting our patients and their families were integrated into our operations at unprecedented rates. We published our findings in the peer-reviewed literature and continually examined processes to deliver better, more personalized customer service. Word spread that we were caring for patients in a bold new way. Our teams were energized to come to work every day because we were improving our patients' lives by offering them innovative treatment options that gave them hope. Through articles and presentations at scientific meetings, we shared our success stories throughout the country and internationally.

KEY TAKEAWAYS

» Begin with a clear, strategically aligned vision to drive transformational change.

» Seek to understand individual expectations, values, and views across generations.

» Ask your team members what they want to maintain or change.

» Motivate your team with individual, meaningful incentives that reflect the true value of the innovation and their unique preferences.

» When viewpoints diverge, respect differences, nurture relationships, and seek the middle ground.

» Remember that some fundamentals remain constant, like the need for your people to feel appreciated, valued, and part of the team.

» Realize that trust, understanding, and respect are always important, as are leaders who express their gratitude for a job well done.

«‹‹‹›››

Meredith Lubitz, vice president of talent management at Dow Jones, writes on empowering the next generation.

As a preeminent media company, we have been facing profound change driven by digital disruption. Few of us could have foretold the exponential growth of accessibility and immediacy of news and information over the past 20 years. The *Wall Street Journal*, our flagship property, has seen seismic change from what was once a niche print publication to an online destination encompassing video, mobile, and social media. With the changing landscape, we realized that our millennial employees would be a vital source of feedback on our new target customer demographic.

As the head of talent management, I cultivate opportunities to build a richer experience by nurturing younger workers' generational demands with such things as internship and job shadowing programs, rotational experiences, and Fun Fridays.

Transitioning from just a "paper" to our present content delivery provider left our company with more trees through which to see the forest, yet in envisioning our company's new challenges, crucial questions emerged: How do we create a greater sense of engagement among these young employees? How do we provide a petri dish for millennials to germinate big ideas that would impact the business in tangible ways?

My team designed a program called Mobile Week. A full five days of interactive sessions, hands-on product demos, and provocative panel discussions emboldening us to think creatively about new business possibilities.

Enter Divya.

Divya, a striking young woman who had previously lived in several countries including Taiwan, Canada, the United States, the United Kingdom, and China, fully engaged in the Mobile

Week experience. She asked a lot of thought-provoking questions. Her inquiring mind and esprit de corps immediately drew me to her.

We met one-on-one shortly after Mobile Week along with her colleague Natalie, a Bronx native and first generation Dominican-American. With their infectious passion and authentic ideas, both realized their reciprocal part to play in helping the organization realize its own goals.

And then it struck me! I immediately connected the dots. These two would dynamically lead a group at the company where millennials within could help "think tank" what Dow Jones should be doing to be more impactful. Together, we turned the key in the ignition on an affinity group called Upstart, with the goal of providing enterprising individuals at Dow Jones an opportunity to engage in what I call the workplace "Millennial 3 C's": Connect, Converse, and Contribute! Topics run the gamut from intrapreneurship, to merging personal and professional development, as well as skills that matter in the workplace today and tomorrow. Thus was the formative genesis of a platform by which millennials had a voice that didn't bind them exclusively to their job title.

By providing a regular forum such as Upstart, Gen Y employees can express themselves and make their mark on the world and Dow Jones can simultaneously benefit from their creative ideas and contributions.

DEVELOPING OUR LEADERSHIP BEHAVIORS

03

The four main qualities discussed in Chapter 2 provide a strong base for the contemporary leader. Focusing on these attributes—trust, confidence, enlightenment, and tenacity—will help you be a distinctive leader and set an example every single day. They will also help you establish yourself among your peers, colleagues, and partners, no matter their level. In every interaction you have, whether one-on-one or in a group, in person or online, you must exude these qualities.

Simply having the traits to be a great leader, however, is not enough if your behavior does not support them. Every leader thinks he or she is trustworthy, confident, enlightened, and tenacious. Consistently showing it through actions is a different level of skill altogether. Without consistent reinforcement of these qualities, with behavior to support them, they will fall flat—and so will you.

The four most important behaviors for leaders are exhibited in the areas of communication, presence, a willingness to try new things, and the ability to help your team members overcome barriers (real or imagined). You cannot passively sit by—you must take steps forward, true action, to ensure the success not only of yourself, but of those you lead as well.

Be Uber-Communicative: Use All Channels to Connect

You may not realize it, but whether verbally or nonverbally, responsive or irresponsive, short- or long-winded, everything you say, and every move you make, communicates a message. It is therefore imperative that no matter what approach you take in communicating a thought, idea, or plan, you must make sure that your message has been received as you intended. Communication as a leader essentially has two purposes:

1. To deliver a message
2. To establish common understanding of the message

In the new world of work, which has constant distraction from our devices and more diverse constituents than ever, it is not enough to send a message and expect that everyone received it in the same way. A fourth revolution leader is responsible for the impact, not just the intent.

We like to use the term "uber-communicative" to describe a type of superior communication incorporating constant updates, feedback, and a clear understanding among all participants in a conversation. Communication is key to an organization's success—it's not enough to simply "communicate openly."

The words you select in any verbal or written exchange are a powerful force: the right ones can help improve a tough situation, the wrong ones can exasperate it beyond repair. Good leaders think through their every word and even rehearse what they will say in their heads before opening their mouths or typing on their keyboards. Jockeying for the mindshare of your audience is a reality in the new world of work. Rehearsing makes it more likely that you will establish connection and attention long enough to make your message heard.

> **"Leaders think they are clear, but they are often not."**

Of course getting and keeping someone's attention isn't always a simple affair. Many times you'll find that it's not just the specifics of what you are trying to communicate that matter, but also how you are communicating them. "Uber-communication" takes this factor into account, making sure you're prepared on all fronts before entering a discussion, giving a presentation, or even sending an e-mail.

It's Not Just What You Say

Communication goes beyond words and includes comportment, posture, clothes, tone of voice, facial expression, and energy level. Experts say 80 percent of what gets across in a discussion comes from your "presence, comportment, and appearance," and the other 20 percent comes from the words you speak (Debra Benton, *How to Think Like a CEO*, Warner Books, 1991). For example, if you hold yourself with an erect bearing, you are likely to seem more relaxed and confident than if you are hunched over. This postures gives the cue that you feel comfortable in the conversation and you believe in the information or sentiment you are expressing. And you relax others. If you walk and talk in a fast-clipped pace, you may come across as aloof, nervous, or not particularly concerned with the conversation. Talking purposefully and slowly will help you explain your point better and show that it is important. If you look a person in the eye and maintain a relaxed, confident facial expression, that person is more likely to pay attention to what you are saying and understand the gravity of the conversation than if you have shifty eyes and a blasé attitude. Keep in mind, you are always communicating beyond your choice of words.

Body language is a real form of communication that is both seen and felt. As corporate office settings begin to change—utilizing open floor plans and open-door policies, for example—there is greater awareness about how your physical actions, or inactions, project messages. When you stop using words, you continue to speak with your body.

Keeping an upward curved mouth with your lips slightly apart is the most important physical act when communicating—that's right, a small smile! The right smile makes your facial expression both confident and modest, and it's possible to hear in the tonality of your voice and sense in the words in an e-mail. Pursed lips and a clinched jaw, however, make you look and sound intimidated, scared, and uncertain. You have to "notify your face" of your intentions

> **"The ideal physical presence for leaders is perfectly relaxed and self-contained."**

so you are able to clearly project confidence in your message. A smile also helps you acknowledge others with a sense of warmth and friendliness. But you must hold this game face whether you are mad or glad. Consistency in comportment breeds confidence and trust in others.

> "If you want to communicate to postmillennials, do it with images. That's how they communicate with each other."

In the past, body language was mostly related to "in-person" communication, but with advances in technology, there are many cases in which you may not be in the same room with a person, but he or she can still observe your posture and facial expressions, such as through video chat services like Skype and FaceTime. Leaders both today and in the future must have a consistent demeanor while still being sensitive and in tune with the interpretation of their physicality. Body language, however, is just one aspect of effective communication.

Clarity and Accommodation

With ever more information out there today that needs to be sorted and prioritized, the opportunities for mistakes, misfires, and misconception of an intended message are many and the ramifications massive. Fourth revolution leaders must therefore be clear, concise, and brief in their directions and responses. They also need to repeat themselves when appropriate. For example, each group or team member needs to hear important information directly from the boss. This means leaders are likely repeating themselves more than they want to, but they must remain patient and avoid exasperation.

Repeating yourself is not about rambling or being verbose. It is about clarification and emphasis and is appropriate whenever you are sending a message that has some complexity or contains a new concept. Repetition and brevity together are a powerful mix for strong communication. Straightforward explanations, patience, and a sincere desire to convey a message help leaders and their staff to connect and understand one another. This type of communication cuts through everyday work-life noise and helps teams focus on completing projects, meeting deadlines, overcoming challenges, and succeeding.

Effective leaders communicate clearly and with reasoning. For example, they provide detailed explanations such as: "This is what needs to get done because of _____. The reason you're the one to do it is _____. The benefit to you is _____. The benefit to the organization is _____. So are you up for the challenge?" Instead of talking about rules, regulations, or political gamesmanship, you need to explain things in a way that people now think. Use imagery, brevity, and a motivating message to be successful as a leader.

You cannot overcommunicate. That might mean using Slack, Skype, e-mail, text, a printed newsletter, phone calls, and town hall meetings to make sure your message is heard loud and clear. Using multiple channels and mediums not only shows that you are a leader who is connected and supportive of both new and traditional types of communication methods, but doing so increases your chances of being heard when working with a wide range of generations and cultures. You have to accommodate others' communication preferences and meet their needs accordingly.

Tell them your preferred style—for example, you may want them to call you in certain situations and e-mail you in others. Be open and honest—if you don't check your voice mail, make sure people know to e-mail you instead. Then ask them their preferred method of communication. Maybe they rely more heavily on an interoffice instant messaging platform than on phone calls and e-mails. Gen X, Y, and Z, for example, infrequently use answering machines and don't necessarily even set up voice mail on their smartphones. You therefore need to be comfortable reaching everyone in the manner that fits their own style and preference. This might mean texting your team to notify them about an e-mail you just sent, or setting up group messaging to stay in touch throughout the day. Sometimes you will have to text information before verbalizing it in an upcoming meeting or conference call. To meet generational needs, your mantra might become, "talk less, text more."

MIND SWITCH FACT

Global nutrition company Herbalife released findings of a survey in 2015 that studied people in their thirties and forties, conducted by market research company Lightspeed GMI. They found that almost 45 percent of the respondents spent eight or more hours a day on digital devices. They were aiming to "assess whether excess use of devices harms the cerebral abilities—whether they are getting digital dementia." Among the survey respondents, apparently 63 percent reported memory loss in their daily lives, 48 percent experienced forgetfulness in the workplace."

Using different technologies to communicate will create a greater impact, but they of course all come with their own particular quirks and pitfalls. For example, a short text message may seem as if the sender is annoyed or not particularly concerned with the details of the message. E-mails are also a hotbed of misunderstanding—a subtle joke or sarcastic comment can be easily misinterpreted, leading to contention and contempt. Geographic and social norms should also be considered. While tech developments have made communication faster and broadly easier, globalization has arguably made it harder, demanding that leaders be inclusive as well as effective in using the tools available. Therefore, no matter the platform, clarity is key.

While using tech-enabled tools to communicate will improve efficiency, reach, and effectiveness, it's also important to get out from behind your device! Walk across the hall and talk face-to-face with members of your team as much as possible. Go out and meet clients and colleagues to better understand where they are coming from and what you can do to help them succeed. In doing so, you will also gain better insight on how to communicate with others in a way that doesn't alienate them. You'll understand how to choose the right words, time your responses, maintain the correct tone, and pepper in humor when appropriate, no matter if you're sitting across from someone or talking with someone from halfway around the world.

> "A subcomponent of communication that I'm working on is to be aware of communication gaps between groups and be the connector between them."

Storytelling Matters

In addition to body language and clear, concise, and accommodating communication methods, leaders must also think about their "forms" of communication. Levity, for example, is a form of communication meant to relax others, reduce your own tension, and allow you to be more candid. Appropriate physical contact—such as a hand on a shoulder to express solidarity when celebrating something—is another form that conveys sincerity, support, and congratulations. Culturally, some people are more comfortable with physical contact, such as those from Latin American countries, and some less. Baby boomers, for example, are generally more receptive to physical contact.

With mixed demographics, a particularly effective form is the telling of stories, examples, or analogies. The greatest leaders throughout history used such forms to communicate instructions, ideas, and values. For example, the Bible and the teachings of Buddha both involve stories and parables. Native Americans teach and correct children through stories, not criticism.

Today's best business leaders use truthful storytelling in their communication as well. For example, when today's leaders are explaining why innovation is imperative, they share failures of their past in enough detail to set the context of urgency and the reality of consequences. They are truthful about the messiness that sometimes happens and don't sugarcoat the missteps. In the past, leaders were more likely to gloss over the failures and stoicism was a behavior that was rewarded. Business leaders that have used truthful storytelling effectively include David Pottruck, the former CEO of Charles Schwab who is known for openly sharing with Fast Company and others his painful experience of losing his job and draws on the Schwab experience in his book about change, *Stacking the Deck*. He is an admirably open and effective storyteller and leader.

To incorporate stories into your communication methods, first set the scene. Next, briefly explain what happened. Lastly, wrap up the story with a moral or the key takeaways that you want the audience to remember. For example, one of Debra's favorite mentors taught her the importance of not deferring to power through the following illustrative story:

> "I had a boss who everyone thought was a real jerk," he said. "He screamed orders, changed his mind, screamed his new orders. People detested working for him. I was young and independent enough so I decided to quit. But first, I wanted to go in and tell him that *he* was the reason why. I screamed a little, then he did, too. So I literally jumped up on the guy's desk and looked at him and said, 'Everyone else feels the same, they just are afraid to come and tell you, but I'm not!' He said, 'They do?' 'Yes, across the board,' I told him. He calmed down and told me to get off the desk and talk, give him the specifics. I did because I didn't care. He said no one had ever given him any feedback like that. After a while, it was getting late and he asked if I would go to dinner with him. I did and I had the first lobster I ever had in my life. I didn't quit. He changed a lot. We remained friends till he died."

If you can incorporate an emotional or physical reaction into the scenario you have chosen—all the better. For example, when Kylie wants to talk with her team about making hard decisions, she draws on her more emotional leadership experiences during the global financial crisis and details true stories of companies that *didn't* make hard decisions about their strategy, staffing, or finances. The result of not making hard decisions meant life or death for their businesses. In her role as a strategist, getting others to think about different scenarios that may play out over the long term, and make decisions accordingly, is difficult, but stories are enormously helpful.

If you have been in a leadership role for some time, use stories that are current and that your audience can relate to. A story about a lauded leader from the past might cause you to be labeled an out-of-touch boomer, but a story about Matthew McConaughey and his cryptic Chrysler television ads might garner more interest. The reverse, however, is also true. If you are a rising leader, read up on business icons and leaders of the past—not only will you learn some lessons, but this will also help you relate across generations. The more you keep your content current, sensational, or memorable, the better your message will be received. For example, if you are in an industry that needs to embrace digital business models, and you are trying to get people to buy into that strategy, look to familiar companies that are making dramatic bets on digital businesses. For example, as we write this book, we would use Walmart's bid for Jet.com as a talking point to get people's attention. Similarly, you must keep *yourself* current and interesting—a behavior we refer to as "dynamic."

Be Dynamic: Enable Change in Yourself and Others

The scientifically oriented definition of dynamic leadership refers to the energy or force that produces motion instead of static. Dynamic leaders move things forward, reduce confusion, and refuse to stagnate. In a fast-moving world full of constant distractions, these leaders move beyond interferences to set the appropriate direction and change when the time is right. Dynamic leaders:

» Excite their staff by consistently introducing new ideas
» Have a creative ability that inspires others
» Bring energy and focus to implementing new ideas
» Change with the times at breakneck speed
» Consider all situations with one eye always looking toward the future
» Are often referred to as charismatic because they model confident behavior

Dynamic leaders in the fourth revolution will attract the most followers. We all want someone to look up to, admire, and emulate. Someone who is energetic, spirited, gutsy, feisty, and maybe a little bit of an ass-kicker.

> **"If you are not moving forward these days, then you are moving backward."**

Whether we call it spunk, or magnetism, or presence, we look for that special something in someone, and when we find it, we try to capture it for ourselves as well. Dynamic leaders, however, are more than just spirited and magnetic—and they are way more than charismatic. They continuously change and advance, behaviors that require substance as well as style. More important, dynamic leaders enable others to reach their goals.

A big part of leadership used to be about change *management*, in which leaders systematically support individuals while an organization, project, or initiative is going through some type of transition. With the pace of demographic flux and technological innovation, however, leadership is now more about change *enablement*. The subtle but important distinction between "enabling change" versus "managing change" recognizes that instead of simply monitoring and smoothing the process of change (change management) you are trying to engage with it and make it happen (change enablement). It is like the difference between following a new recipe because someone has told you it is going taste great versus going to the fresh food market and selecting ingredients you have never tried and finding a recipe to bring them together into something delicious.

Constant innovation is imperative in today's business environment and enabling change—in processes, culture, product development—is part of being a dynamic leader. Some leaders are naturally endowed with this ability, but for others it takes focus and determination. Looking forward to what's on the horizon and realizing the urgency of the changing marketplace is the key to becoming a dynamic leader—"speed" is the name of the game.

MIND SWITCH FACT

In 2015 in Australia, Edelman Borland conducted a survey on GE's behalf—GE Global Barometer 2016. Of 109 Australian business executives and 106 members of the informed public, they found 69 percent among both groups were excited about the new digital-industrial era—compared with 61 percent of execs and 65 percent of citizens globally.

New Realities of Competition

Dynamic leaders work to speed up processes and produce a competitive advantage. Globalization and the availability of faster and more powerful automation tools means competitors are everywhere and they are not as cut-and-dried as they once were. For example, as we were writing this book, Apple made a sizeable investment ($1 billion) in Didi Chuxing Technology Co., a ride-hailing company that is estimated to complete around 10 times more rides per day than Uber. In essence, by investing in China's largest player in the ride-hailing industry, Apple has entered the transportation industry.

In the meantime, General Motors is a fairly large investor in Lyft, yet another ride-hailing service. Furthermore, both Apple and GM are looking to get ahead of the curve on autonomous driving. We think it is safe to say that even in 2010, just six years before we wrote this book, Apple would never have been seen as a competitor with GM, but as worlds converge, neat industry segmentations with clear competitors are fading quickly. Technology is making product and service adaptations possible at greater speeds than ever before while helping companies enter new industries at a rate never seen before.

MIND SWITCH FACT

Fear of becoming obsolete, or FOBO, is becoming a very real distraction for individuals and companies. As written in the *Harvard Business Review* (2013) by Mark Bonchek, "As individuals, we're afraid of being left behind in our careers. A recent survey by Oxford Economics found employees' top concern is that their position might change or become obsolete. Half believe their current skills won't be needed in three years. And the fear has spread to the C-suite: a study by Adobe found that 40 percent of marketing executives feel the need to reinvent themselves but only 14 percent feel they know how."

It is not only large companies that are taking on new categories of products and services to compete with historically disparate industries. Start-ups tend to find a market need and quickly develop a following, creating disruption based on edgy branding, a superior customer experience, or better digital friendly interfaces. Such small companies can establish a foothold before incumbents even have time to react. For example, the eyewear company Warby Parker, which started in a Philadelphia apartment in 2010, launched a disruptive online service in which the company will send customers five pairs of glasses to try out at home before they actually buy them. Just six years later, Warby Parker is valued at over $1 billion.

JD.com is another perfect example. The company was originally a small chain of retail stores in China selling a very specific line of consumer electronics products ("magneto-optical"). During the SARS (severe acute respiratory syndrome) outbreak in 2003, however, JD.com transitioned to an online business because fewer people were visiting stores due to health concerns. They didn't want to catch the dreaded SARs by interacting in person with others. JD.com is now one of the largest online retailers in China—sometimes referred to as a "future Amazon"—selling all manner of products. In 2014, the company was valued at more than $40 billion when it listed on NASDAQ.

To survive among these disruptions and the blurring lines of competition, leaders must be willing to change and adapt. They do not want to find themselves waking up to a Kodak or Blockbuster situation in which they stubbornly produced their products and iterated instead of looking forward. Dynamic leaders do not let a person, company, or disruption come along and recreate their destiny for them—they change with the trends, innovate, and lead their team through the accompanying challenges. To do so, they must be extremely flexible.

MIND SWITCH FACT

In Australia, 89 percent of business leaders surveyed in the GE Global Innovation Barometer in 2016 believe "that many businesses will face 'digital Darwinism' due to disruption in coming years. Only Brazil, with a score of 90 percent, outdoes Australia (barely) in this anxiety."

Source: www.gereports.com.

Dynamic leaders adapt to new technologies and pivot with changing markets and customer attitudes and desires. The term "pivot," popularized by *The Lean Startup* author Eric Reis, is used almost as a war cry for innovation teams in different industries and companies, including legendary behemoths like GE and Intuit, around the world. The definition of pivot, according to Reis, is "structured course correction designed to test a new fundamental hypothesis about the product, strategy, and engine of growth." His methodology is both logical and inspiring and one we will likely see more widely adopted in the new world of work. A good example of a pivot is the well-covered change in direction that Netflix took early in its journey to move away from DVDs by mail and into digital delivery. At the time, it may have seemed too early, but it had done its market analysis and the rest is history.

Challenges to Being Dynamic

Being dynamic is a particularly high bar for many leaders to reach. We are all on a continuum of comfort with change and an ability to adapt. Frankly, though, it can be exhausting! Dynamic leaders must be savvy beyond reproach—what we like to call "omni-savvy"—in person, online, and across disciplines. They must be willing to leave their comfortable domain of specialization and embrace a sense of business savvy, tech savvy, emotional intelligence, and cultural fluency.

As some people say, the corporate ladder is more like a jungle gym these days. Constant change will keep leaders fitter than ever, but their ability to change at the right times, breaking from convention and static inaction, will determine whether they sink or swim. Speed and change enablement will remain essential for leaders to stay ahead of where they need to be and build an enduring career, team, and business. Of course, it doesn't matter if you're an assistant or a CEO, change can be scary. Keeping the right attitude, however, will go a long way to handling change, as will the willingness to open yourself up to others and have some fun.

Be Playful: Have Some Fun and Try New Things

Leading others takes a spirit and boldness to make decisions and follow through with your actions. You need to try new things and push boundaries. You also need to know when to have fun and when to be serious, when to joke around and when to be stern. Being playful is perhaps the most controversial of the behaviors we believe make for exceptional

> **"Leaders bring the weather every day—they determine if it is going to be stormy or sunny, and the best ones make it sunny most of the time."**

leaders. But increasingly, as our professional and personal lives blend into each other, it is important to bring levity to the workplace, while making it enjoyable for others to be around you.

Today, being fully invested in your job takes time and effort away from home and family, hobbies, and friends. It is a reality that many people's working lives have extended in both hours on the job and years on the job—retirement ages have increased due to financial necessity, changing pension and social security systems, and personal choice. While 40-hour workweeks were the starting point for most professionals in the 1970s, many white-collar professionals have since seen their work commitments balloon up to 60 hours or more per week. Their digital devices—smartphones, laptops, iPads, and so on—have become their masters, and they are constantly connected to the office. True escapes from professional demands are hard to come by.

Resulting from this reality, increasingly, people don't have the goal of work-life balance; they just have the goal of living a life that is as fulfilling as possible irrespective of how different activities fall into traditional buckets of work or play. Understanding this can help you unblock your team and motivate them to give more. For example, members of Gen Y are generally unwilling to give up important things that traditionally fall into the domain of their personal lives to "get ahead." They tend to be more minimalist than earlier generations, just doing their job and no more (especially if they feel they aren't valued). Introducing a type of playfulness, however, will help create a more positive, productive environment. Your team will be more relaxed and you'll be able to connect with them on a level that you had not in the past. Whether it be hosting a foosball tournament once a month or incorporating gamification into the workplace, anything that honors the realization that work and play have merged somewhat can help engage across the generations.

Many tech companies and start-ups have already learned that they have to incorporate "playful symbols" at work. For example, LinkedIn headquarters in California reportedly has a room for musical instruments to be played by employees, and Google headquarters in Zurich has a slippery slide to the canteen. This relaxed, fun environment may be required to attract highly sought-after talent in the fourth revolution. More established companies with traditional corporate structures are now catching up and following suit as well. For example, CNN was one of the early companies to introduce "Play Well Stairs" into its headquarters in Atlanta. According to one of its wellness consultants interviewed on the topic, "We transformed the 36 step-staircase into a fully working 'Piano Staircase.' The staircase is wrapped to resemble a giant piano keyboard, and each step or 'key' plays a note as someone steps on it. We also installed a real-time step

> **"Realize that your priorities are not necessarily their priorities."**

counter that shows how many steps employees have taken since the installation. Additionally, a live webcam is set up so that employees from our other office locations can watch a live stream of the action through our company intranet."

Making Work Fun

It can be daunting to approach the topic of being playful since leaders from earlier generations typically did not have that experience throughout their careers. Their peers are also still working in their "tried and true" ways such as wearing ties, maintaining nine-to-five hours, and hosting happy hours as the only outlet for team bonding. They may not see the demands of the future yet. However, as a leader, basing the idea in the context of being willing to try new things should soften the message and hopefully dispel some skepticism. Who wants to be the one unwilling to try new things? In a public setting, no one wants to admit to being a curmudgeon, and you can use that to your advantage.

An easy way for leaders to inject some fun into their office culture is through something everyone likes: food. Find out what your team and colleagues like to eat and have a party catered with their favorite foods. Make sure to present options that fit the taste and health interests of your teams, not your own taste. If hummus and pita bread, chocolate-covered raspberries, and granola bars are what people like to eat, have those instead of the bland suggestions from corporate catering companies.

> **"I'm more than willing to do what is needed when it is required, but I still want a life—more than my parents had."**

Even better than a cookie-cutter approach to being playful is instituting something that reflects the unique culture of your team or company. For example, apparel company Quicksilver encourages surfing breaks. Zappos apparently holds regular pajama parties. Google lets people expense up to $500 in takeout food while they are on maternity leave. And Citigroup announced a new plan to keep millennials happy: give them a year off. According to the *Wall Street Journal*, as of March 2016, Citigroup had announced a program for chosen incoming analysts where they can take a service year and go work for a charitable organization from an approved list. During this time, they will receive 60 percent of their pay.

Whether it's a pizza party or an excursion to the beach, you need to first find out what your team values and what they believe will liven up the potential drudgery of everyday office life. Let your multigenerational teams explain to you what they see as "balance" in their work life and personal life. Get a feeling for what they consider "fun"—not everyone will be interested in a group skydiving trip, for example. Understanding your team both as a whole and as individuals will help you become a more well-rounded leader. Learning to be more flexible in your thought processes and actions, on the job or at home, will get you one step closer to a full leadership mind switch.

"I try to listen to their requests for time with family and/or giving back to the community and work with them whenever possible. I adjust to their lifestyle, not the other way around always."

Good Humor and Nature

Playful leaders are usually good-humored. Humor helps humanize you and makes any problem seem smaller. A confident leader tries to make people laugh, chuckle, snort, smile, and generally feel good. Considering the amount of time you spend with your colleagues, why not try to make it as enjoyable as possible? No matter how great a leader you are, you are placed in numerous uncomfortable, stressful, and difficult situations every week. To get over them, it is necessary to have a good sense of humor and a willingness to laugh. For example, producer and director Ricky Gervais, says, "That's what laughter is for—to get you through stuff." And another Brit, the late Prime Minister Winston Churchill, said, "A joke is a very serious thing. If you make someone laugh, you give them a little vacation."

Being "good-humored," however, doesn't necessarily mean telling jokes. Bonds are created when people share an understanding of some absurdity—and as we all know, absurdity abounds in any business—or a surprise that results in laughter. Your own version of good humor might be making people smile often and creating an open environment where people are more likely to laugh. You don't have to constantly crack jokes, and you don't want to verge on the edge of annoyance.

Playful leaders are never frosty; they are vigilant against edginess in their voice and facial expressions. They are inclusive by making sure there is some common understanding of the words, images, experiences, or emotions they are expressing. They also know that humor can be dangerous. While it can open minds and bring people together, it can also close minds and tear people apart if it is, or is perceived as, pejorative, sexist, racist, insulting, ridiculing, or plain mean-spirited. Obviously you need to always avoid any humor of this kind.

Building a Playful Environment

Great leaders plan their "spontaneity" by being intentional about their playful actions, while still making them look like the moment just arose. For example, giving everyone the afternoon to go to the golf driving range when a particularly lucrative sales order arrives (which they had planned out in advance) in a less busy time of year or month. Another example is letting others help them with comic relief at work, like sharing a cartoon from *The New Yorker*, referencing a line from a sitcom, or showing a movie trailer at their desk and joining in as the leader to show that we can all enjoy more playful moments in the new world of work—as long as they are appropriate moments that don't offend or exclude.

Making the mind switch to being a more playful leader will open completely unexpected paths of opportunity. Your teams will find you more approachable and, as a result, will be more likely to raise questions, thoughts, or ideas that they may have previously been hesitant to propose for fear of being shut down. Creating a more playful environment for your team to interact within will enhance collaboration opportunities, and smiling and laughing with others will create bonds that are unique and harder to break than those based on shared goals alone.

We need to be clear that "playfulness" is not about frivolity, it is about building a creative and positive environment. It is also about respecting the fact that work lives now often blur the lines with personal lives. Being a playful, albeit results-oriented, leader acknowledges that many workers of the future aren't there just to climb the ladder, or through the jungle gym, but to add to their bucket list of life experiences and adventures.

Actively "Unblock" Others: Free Your People

Effective leadership is selfless: it's about growing others, not just yourself. Great leaders provide their people with the tools to succeed, offer support so their efforts flourish, encourage risk taking, and keep tabs on the progress along the way. They empower people to grow, to do more, and to be more. To do so, they must help remove barriers to progress. These barriers include legacy thinking, risk aversion, overly structured thinking, and tunnel vision based on "groupthink." In addition to these types of barriers, people tend to "block" themselves with their own limiting attitudes. External forces also play a role: people can block others due to misaligned attitudes, age, race, gender, and more. Leaders must therefore help their team members, managers, and colleagues "unblock" and rise above these imposed limitations.

The concept of *unblocking* reflects hundreds of conversations we had with rising leaders who want to contribute more to the overall success of their organization or company. Yet they feel blocked by antiquated processes, others who are in roles above them, or attitudes that are not moving forward with the times. People of all ages, but especially the rising generations, want to be empowered, authorized, and enabled to fix the inefficiencies their predecessors created. Unblocking people and processes requires you to find out what motivates and inspires your team. If you don't, they will walk.

Unblocking leaders are thoughtful and positive; they encourage their people to stretch themselves in new ways and inspire them to gather experience that is beneficial both personally and professionally. They encourage not discourage. For example, such a leader may offer an opportunity to a rising star on her team to get involved in an M&A transaction even though the person hasn't done it before. This will help the rising star to develop new skills and a new network of people. In the past, such developmental opportunities were probably reserved for the most senior employees. Unblocking leaders challenge their highest potential team members regularly and give clues, but not the answers, to the puzzles yet to be solved. They seek and give feedback to help others continuously improve.

They also put effort into their team consistently. Instead of ignoring, they

"To get things accomplished you have to collaborate through others."

engage. They avoid making people feel invisible. This doesn't mean trying to please everyone—we all know that's near impossible. Instead, true leaders choose their priorities carefully while using communication tools wisely in order to make everyone feel part of the mission, plan, or process.

Accepting and Embracing Everyone on Your Team

Helping others unblock is not necessarily an easy process. The first step can be a hurdle, but it's important to overcome it early on. To be an admired leader, your mindset has to be one void of judgment toward character or the motives of your diverse workforce. Due to our frame of reference and our own experiences, we all bring personal thoughts to the office about other people we work with. If any of these are negative, however, we need to overcome them—the desire to create an environment for success and innovation should be our main concern. Accepting others for who they are and what they bring to the table as capable human beings will help them believe in their own worth, talents, and strengths. If they know you "have their back," they will be more willing to work hard and succeed.

Unblocking leaders tell their teams they believe in them (and then they actually do believe in them!). These leaders connect with each team member on a personal level. They make eye contact and use their names—and their dogs' names. Great leaders take the time to learn about their individual staff members and colleagues, their hobbies, the music they like, and the sports they enjoy. They remain nonjudgmental, act genuinely, and give others respect. In turn, this accepting attitude garners respect and displays a leader's authenticity.

Accepting and embracing your team will especially be important when you need to help team members overcome disagreements. It is important to attack the *issue* not the person and keep no record of grievances, in other words to discourage a tit-for-tat environment where mistakes or arguments are saved away to be raised later. This prevents the potential of blocked communication and fractured relationships, which can hinder a team's performance. Embracing your team also goes a long way toward empowering them.

Empowering Your Team

The second step to helping your team unblock is to empower the team members quickly, even if they don't feel entirely ready. Giving promotions, money, and higher titles to younger employees can seem daunting and risky. You must have courage and trust your people and your ability to appraise their performance—it will be absolutely necessary to recruit and retain the best talent in a fast-moving new world of work.

The buzzword around this act is "juniorization," which has been popularized in investment banking circles in recent years and refers to the substitution of experienced employees with more junior ones. Deploying juniorization may keep your team young, energetic, and potentially ahead of the curve, but a possible negative side effect includes potentially pushing aside more seasoned team members sooner than is optimal. Empowerment is not simply for younger staff. You must also support seasoned people, and make objective decisions on the best people and processes to help the business thrive.

In Brooks Brothers factories, for example, over 50 percent of the employees are over 55 years old. According to an article on Brooks Brothers management in business trades, "They are more experienced, work faster, work more accurately, and yes, get paid more money." The management team apparently believes this isn't just an issue of age, but of how that age group feels empowered to perform their work—they are given the right tools, strong incentives, and respect on the job. They are also given the freedom to do their work without constant intervention by the higher-ups.

> **"Young people today want to know 'What's in it for me?' and 'What will I learn from it?'"**

By empowering your team to let them make more of their own decisions, they will find their own ways of overcoming barriers. As an effective leader, it's important to facilitate on-the-job learning. Instead of constant micromanaging that kills an individual's feelings of ownership over a project or job, try to direct less, and put more faith in your team's talents and capabilities. Step in when a problem or situation arises in which there is no other option aside from intervention, but otherwise let the network of teams and individuals collaborate and solve problems for themselves. Today, leadership is not about creating your own legacy; it's about empowering others and teaching them how to lead.

Pat 'Em on the Back

Mark Twain once wrote, "I can live for two months on a good compliment." This comment resonates with so many people today who are starved for recognition and direction. It is no longer acceptable for leaders to have negative attitudes like one boss we spoke with who said, "I don't ever compliment outright. Them not getting fired is their compliment." Even more telling is that numerous C-level executives we talked to admitted that they simply weren't skilled at giving recognition. "I personally don't need it, so I'm not very good at giving it," they profess. The problem, however, is that recognition is integral to performance, especially when employees are feeling stuck or facing a particularly difficult issue that they need help with. Today, recognition is not a nicety, it's a necessity, and that's why it is the third step to helping your people unblock.

Make sure to provide your staff with constant recognition for innovative thinking and actions. Sharing frequent "pats on the back," figuratively and literally, in public and in private, is more important than ever. Consider highlighting positive customer comments cc'd to the team, or make some small gestures like mailing a gift card for a popular restaurant to the partner (or sometimes the parent) of the deserving employee. Another good thing to do is reinforce good behavior openly among your staff by asking for help on projects and initiatives in front of them. They want to know what they are doing is correct and important. Building their self-confidence will help them face and overcome the many

> "Not every boss gives helpful feedback. Some have the approach, 'Don't expect me to like you. . . . Don't expect me to like your work. . . . And do expect to be criticized.'"

obstacles that could potentially block their success and progress every day.

Providing recognition is a debt you
owe to the people who are making a
true effort at work and performing
effectively. If you reinforce the actions
that you want to see, you will likely get
more of the same. If you don't acknowl-
edge them, they won't know your degree of satisfaction.
Naturally you praise what you admire the most, adding your
reason for it. On occasion, give your people a little more
praise than is their due.

> **"If I don't tell my team they are doing a good job, they think I don't care."**

Also keep in mind that recognition in the contemporary
business world needs to be immediate. Gen X, Y, and Z want
instant gratification (well, regardless of age, honestly, who
doesn't?), instant rewards, and real-time feedback. They also
don't appreciate delays. Pamper, compliment, fluff their
feathers, and make them feel important when you can. Even
if you didn't, or currently don't, get the same type of recognition from up above you, your job as a leader is to provide it to
your people.

A pay raise is one way a boss frequently thinks to provide
recognition. But people need to be appreciated in different
ways. One female executive told me,
"I was ready to quit because I wasn't
receiving recognition. They just keep
throwing more money at me. But that's
not what I work for alone." By not receiving that recognition, she felt she was
being undervalued, which then affected her performance.
It was more difficult for her to overcome obstacles, and she
found herself blocked at almost every turn. Recognizing her

> **"Just be brief, honest, timely, and specific. Note it to others, then back it up."**

accomplishments publicly, expressing that she was doing a great job, and supporting her in her efforts would have gone a long way to helping her move past the roadblocks. Not only would this contribute to her personal success, but to that of the team and the overall company as well.

The Mind Switch on Our Leadership Behaviors

In addition to the four main qualities discussed in Chapter 2—trust, confidence, enlightenment, and tenacity—there are four main behaviors that are essential to the leadership mind switch: being uber-communicative, being dynamic, acting playfully, and helping others unblock. These actions are necessary for anyone looking to stay ahead of the trend and lead across generations and style during the fourth industrial revolution. Behavior leading to impact is believed; well-meaning intent, not so much. Ambitious, hardworking people emulate good leaders. Your attitude combined with behavior set the example you want to see in your people.

STORIES FROM THE ROAD

Tom O'Malley, former president of Vivendi Entertainment, a film, television, DVD, and digital distributor, writes about communicating across functions.

A manager must understand the environment his or her leader operates in. If he doesn't, a likely gap, a dysfunction, develops and the manager is apt to be on the losing end. Let's call it the stakeholder gap.

This gap occurs when a leader fails to effectively educate a manager on the stakeholder forces whirling in the leader's sphere that through power and influence shape the organization's priorities and culture.

Stakeholders are those who have influence on, or authority over, what leaders and managers do. They are people or groups that leaders and managers serve, or interact with in important ways. Note: stakeholders have their own agendas and priorities that directly and indirectly influence the agendas and priorities of leaders. And the composition and nature of stakeholders is very different for leaders than for managers. This reality creates different operating environments for each. Different worlds.

The leader's world is where the most important company decisions are debated and decided: strategies, priorities, policies, culture, and business practices. The leader's world is rendered complex, contradictory, and political by the nature of the stakeholders they serve.

Since the manager doesn't live in the leader's world, his own assumptions about that world can be faulty. From a distance it may appear as one thing—up close it can be something very different.

A resulting leadership challenge ensues: How can a leader successfully educate a manager on the dynamics of a leader's world as influenced by his stakeholders?

Let's focus in on the manager's world first. By design, junior and middle level managers have a few stakeholders that largely exist at their own level. For example, a freight manager may have these stakeholders that influence his actions and motivations: his boss, the freight carriers, a warehouse manager, a customer service manager, and his staff.

Conversely, his leader, the senior VP of operations, has a much larger and more complex stakeholder profile. His includes his own reporting departments of manufacturing, distribution, and customer service; the company's president; and heads of the other functional areas: sales, marketing, strategy, R&D, finance, human resources, and legal. Add to that list customers, suppliers, internal and external auditors, trade associations—the list is extensive.

Stakeholders influence the priorities and overall approach leaders and managers take in performing their tasks. In our example, the manager and the leader both work in the common vertical of operations; however, the influencing forces each faces are vastly different.

A stakeholder gap between a leader and his manager will likely arise when a consistent pattern of behavior and events occurs over time as follows: A manager begins to experience frustration related to resistance or rejection of his ideas and priorities (common in business). His reaction is to appeal to his boss for support and advice. The leader, however, repeatedly chooses not to comprehensively engage his manager's frustrations. Stylistically his engagement level is detached, general, brief, dry facts—devoid of the color and texture essential for the manager to truly understand that the leader's stakeholder environment is beyond the manager's authority, where decisions are made that affect the quality of the manager's work experience and performance.

Without a clear understanding of how and why the forces in the leader's world are impacting the manager's world, the manager is deprived of proper career development. His effort and performance receives flawed feedback in the form of half-truths rising from the distorted echo of his own narrow environment. And a half-truth is no better than a full lie. Rejection and defeat grows heavy without the liberating act of an adequate explanation. The leader tells the manager "what" but not "why." Ultimately, the manager reasons that his leader does not support him. His leader is now part of the problem. A stakeholder gap is born.

It is precisely because a manager and leader's stakeholder world and related influences are so different that contextual communication from a leader is so necessary. And the best leaders, as a rule, share (with exceptions for confidentiality and such) with their managers the high-level forces at play: conflicting priorities, multidimensional implications for decisions, limits of political capital, coalition building, and the magic and mystery of the internal sell.

Candid and comprehensive disclosure of the leader's world and its impact on the manager can help avoid a stakeholder gap and its related dysfunction. And of course the benefits are real.

The manager gains an enriched perspective for the real forces that influence a company's action and behavior; a more accurate read of cause and effect sharpens his judgment, and he is less inclined to take disappointments personally since he is privy to conflicting agendas and priorities within the company. He matures from the rigidity of his parochial concerns. His orientation becomes more "we" than "I." Rejection and defeat now come with meaning and context. They feel entirely different. The manager understands more clearly the forces that actually shape the organization that he aspires to one day shape himself.

Leaders must be reminded to constantly educate managers about the stakeholders in the leader's world and the complex environment in which the company is shaped and steered, and the related impact on the manager's experience.

《《〈〉》》

Margaret Molloy, global CMO at Siegel+Gale, writes about influencing in times of change and accountability in the digital age.

When Margaret Molloy joined brand strategy firm Siegel+Gale as global CMO, she recognized that industrywide the agency-client dynamic was undergoing a significant transformation. On the demand side, clients had more choices and buying cycles were more compressed. On the supply side, agency talent had more opportunities to practice their individual crafts. Margaret decided that it would be beneficial to both clients and internal colleagues to build the profile of Siegel+Gale and its thought leaders. Her marketing team needed to implement a content marketing strategy to harness the firm's views and creative chops. From the outset, Margaret and her team appreciated that the majority of professionals' time was consumed with billable client deliverables, and that motivating colleagues to produce content presented a challenge. To overcome this, the marketing team met with individual practices and presented their content marketing plan. They outlined the potential benefits and the specific role that every practice had in driving success. This deliberate approach enabled Margaret's team to persuade and motivate thought leaders and to identify champions across all levels and disciplines.

WHY IT MATTERS

In the digital age, companies seeking to hire a branding partner are increasingly evaluating the thought leadership of the professionals at the firm. This meant the content marketing strategy needed to harness the intellectual rigor and creativity of Siegel+Gale on a wide range of topics. It had to demonstrate the value of the firm's capabilities and the relevance of its perspectives on branding. Siegel+Gale already had a strong viewpoint on the value of applying simplicity to brand experience. The opportunity, therefore, was to bring that to life in the content.

However, the content creation process needed to be streamlined and as easy as possible for billable professionals, so the marketing team developed guidelines for blogging and bylines—providing thought leaders with a foundation to efficiently codify their points of view. The team also hosted "lunch and learns" to educate everyone about distributing the company's content through LinkedIn and other social platforms. The marketing team shared the content with existing and prospective clients and integrated it into the new business and pitch process. Margaret's vision was to differentiate Siegel+Gale as a modern branding firm in the eyes of clients and new hires alike.

WHAT WAS THE RESULT?

Siegel+Gale team members were inspired to see their thought leadership in top-tier publications and on the firm blog. They were acknowledged for their participation via firm-wide announcements—e.g., the co-CEOs acknowledged active contributors during quarterly town hall meetings. New content also was showcased on screens throughout the office to celebrate contributors. The marketing team developed and shared suggested social posts for newly created content, enabling everyone to amplify their colleagues' content. As a result, the content marketing initiative triggered more active participation across the entire firm on social media. Siegel+Gale experienced record interest from prospective clients, which translated into new business for the firm. This multifaceted content marketing program elevated the profile of the firm, making it a compelling workplace for top branding talent and a world-class branding partner for clients.

As Margaret reflected on the program, she highlighted the importance of developing a focused plan including clear roles and responsibilities for everyone involved. She underlined that an essential success factor was accountability for the plan and a commitment to driving it to completion.

GOOD LEADERS START AS GOOD FOLLOWERS

04

In addition to asking hundreds of Gen X and Gen Y rising leaders about what they want in a boss or manager, we also researched what current, established leaders want in up-and-comers. One question we regularly asked was, "What makes you want to *invest* in an individual?" By using the word "invest," we meant the willingness to identify, seek out, help, sponsor, mentor, elevate, and empower others. We were eager to unpack when and why these leaders celebrate certain people by giving them opportunities and resources before, or instead, of others.

The main headline from this research is that to become an exceptional leader, you must first master the practice of being a good follower. Our hundreds, if not thousands, of conversations with successful executives revealed that people's ability to follow others is an accurate indicator of their future success in a leadership role. Being a good follower doesn't mean losing your independence or desire to lead, it simply means being humble in your approach to learning from others and establishing a career in which you are viewed positively.

> "I'll tell you straight out. What I want in young people is more self- and situational awareness. I also want consistency in good behavior, more decisiveness, more ambition, and less caution."

Regardless of where you are in your career, there is always someone in your organization whose job description it is to consider whether or not you will become future top talent. An effective leader, however, makes sure that everybody gets the opportunity to "shine up" and be given a chance to exhibit their potential. Helping to make leaders out of others is a fundamental job and requirement of any leader; that has not, and will not, change irrespective of technology or demographics. But it is up to rising leaders to decide whether to seize that opportunity—this is where good following comes into play.

According to our research, good followers:

» Have an impeccable work ethic
» Are trustworthy
» Show self-confidence but zero arrogance
» Are easy to be around

You will notice some similarities between these characteristics and the leadership qualities discussed in Chapter 2.

There is good reason for this: becoming a great leader is an evolving process that starts early in your career when you first become part of a team. While the traits may be similar, however, the stakes are different. As a follower you are constantly observing and taking in directions with little risk and much upside. As the leader, every move you make has implications for those around you and there is less room for error.

An Impeccable Work Ethic

T. Boone Pickens is no stranger to a strong work ethic. As an American business mogul, financier, and chairman of the BP Capital Management hedge fund, Pickens has spent his six-decade-long career discovering what it takes to be at the head of the pack. When interviewed by Julia La Roche for *Business Insider*, Pickens attributed his success, and that of others, to skill and relentless effort. He stated, "work ethic is the backbone of success as far as I'm concerned. . . . If you want to be a lawyer, geologist, or a nurse, work ethic comes first. Everything else falls into place." (*I Asked Legendary Tycoon T. Boone for Financial Advice—His Answer Was Surprisingly Simple*, Julia LaRoche, Businessinsider.com, 2015.) This is one of the time-tested leadership traits that we expect to carry over to the fourth revolution, and it starts well before you are in formal leadership positions.

Your work ethic is essential to your success as a follower and a leader. When it comes to getting hired or promoted to a leadership role, you want to be the best candidate for the job, not the "least worst" choice. You have to be willing to

> **"It requires zero talent to be on time, be prepared, put energy in, have a good attitude, and do more than asked of."**

put in the effort to achieve your goals and go beyond the typical boundaries. It's important to pursue "stretch" opportunities and sometimes bite off more than you think you can chew.

Leaders want followers who they believe can surpass expectations and create positive energy and change within an organization. We have never heard of a hiring manager or promotion panel that seeks out people who shirk responsibility or avoid hard work. Nor will we ever hear of this—it simply won't happen.

A strong work ethic, however, is not only about the effort you put forward. It is also about your reliability, attention to quality, and willingness to do whatever it takes to help your team, and your leader, succeed. An impeccable work ethic means you are consistent and unwavering in your delivery and effort to deliver. To do so, you must equally maintain focus at the office whether you're stressed out with a seemingly unending number of responsibilities or having a quiet day or week. You don't want to become known as the worker-bee who is hanging around the water cooler or staring out the window and off into space.

> **"Two things I dislike: When your mom calls me to find out why I gave you a bad performance review. And when you tell me, 'I don't know.' I need you to say, 'I don't know, but I'll find out.'"**

Instead, you want to show others that you can manage your responsibilities, remain dedicated, and get results. They have to know that they can count on you to help move a project or plan toward success. If you take the initiative when others hold back, step up to bat when others steer clear of a difficult job, and volunteer when your peers and colleagues hide in their cubicles, your leaders will help you move up through the ranks. You can also vocalize your commitment to your leaders by responding to their requests with a simple, "I've got this," or "Consider it done." (Then, of course, you must do it.) People will empower you with responsibility and authority if you give them reason to. They will give you progressively harder tasks as you raise their expectations, which you then must continue to strive to surpass.

It's also important to demonstrate the value that you bring to a team. You don't need to be the smartest person in the room, but it is good to find a niche in which you can excel. Familiarize yourself with ideas that your group collectively knows little about. Learn about concepts from outside of your company or team that might benefit everyone together. Most important, become good at tasks or processes that are important to success for the overall group you work with. When you know, or can provide, something of value you are in turn more highly valued.

"You work on average 41.5 hours a week. If you continue that you won't stand out. . . . I understand that you don't want to make the same sacrifices your parents made. . . . But when we are in succession planning meetings examining the pipeline that we want to grow we look at you as maxed out, showing no hunger or ambition. It would be so easy for you to stand out from the rest if you put more interest in embracing control of your career."

While the number of hours put into a project may reflect a great work ethic, the way you consistently behave is truly what matters most. This behavior can't be faked because it is a continuous process, not a point in time. If you stick with it, people around you will spontaneously comment on your performance—whether in meetings behind closed doors or in a public setting—saying things like, "She is so reliable and works tirelessly to deliver." For those people who just work hard when it suits them, the compliments will be noticeably different. The episodic hard worker will be praised for the exception (not the norm), with a comment like, "He *actually* worked pretty hard on that project, and it shows."

To avoid falling into the "episodic hard worker" category, you must actively pursue opportunities. As Colin Shaw, founder and CEO of Beyond Philosophy—the first customer experience consultancy and training company in the world—says, "The starting gun is silent. . . . There is no point waiting for someone or something to show you the way." Don't waste your time waiting for someone to involve you in a project or process—if you do, then it might never happen. Take the first step, make the first move, and ask your leaders how you can be involved. In fact, showing interest and asking thoughtful questions signals your desire to be part of the team and displays your overall work ethic.

> "If I'm on vacation, take on my leadership role yourself. Rise to the occasion versus slowing down and having a 'while the cats away the mice will play' mindset. That shows me what you're made of."

Stay Involved by Asking Questions

Hard workers ask questions because they want to learn as much as they can about their position, profession, company, and industry. They want to understand what goes into certain processes and what is necessary to help the team succeed. Most every conversation can start with one of these words: who, what, when, where, why, or how. A particularly important question that shows you care about a strong work ethic is, "What are your expectations of me?" If you can internalize these expectations, you won't just have the opportunity to meet them, but also to exceed them.

When you ask questions, you better understand other people's perspectives, which can help you look at problems and solutions from different angles. The responses you receive may result in considering problems backward, from "finish to start" instead of "start to finish," or lead you to think about all the reasons something can be done, as compared to *can't* be done. You'll find that people with experience, even if totally unrelated to the subject, can provide enlightening opinions. As long as you avoid narrow thinking and consider workable answers to each problem, you're likely to get good results and improve your overall problem-solving ability.

One particularly astute, hardworking young woman we spoke with during our research told us that she regularly asked senior staff, upper level managers, and other superiors questions in order to understand their perspectives. Most of these leaders were older than she was, and she wanted to have real conversations with them in hopes they'd open up and provide her with knowledge and alternate ways to think about things. Though she believes that many younger workers think they can't relate to older staff, and therefore don't try, she takes the opposite approach. (It also doesn't hurt that she employs humor and jokes during these conversations.) You can bet that her boss takes notice and realizes that she's going the extra mile to further improve her work and herself. It doesn't take an exorbitant amount of effort to set herself apart from others who don't bother asking questions or are fearful of doing so. Also, the use of humor improves receptivity of the inquiry and even allows her to push back in a pleasantly assertive manner to learn even more.

Being able to communicate with your boss, and boss's boss, is one of the best determinants of a successful series of promotions and raises. Make it easy for people to get to you and hear back from you, and communicate by listening more than talking. (Not sure if it is a coincidence or not, but "listen" and "silent" have the same letters in each word.) Of course, don't just ask questions, get answers, and then disappear. You'll only be able to exhibit your work ethic, and your desire to learn and grow into a leader, by putting the knowledge you've gained into consistent action. People don't want to waste time providing you with important information, thoughts, or ideas if you're just going to turn around and throw them in the trash. As a good follower, your leaders need to trust that you'll apply what you've learned every day. They need to trust that your work ethic will remain intact. Simply put: they need to trust you.

"Don't be intentionally or unintentionally unclear."

Trusted and Trustworthy

As discussed in Chapter 2, one of the four main leadership qualities is staying trustworthy beyond reproach, or as we call it, "true blue." Before you are promoted to a leadership role, you must first exhibit this quality. People want to know that when left to your own devices you can make the right choices. The last thing the higher-ups want is to be stuck worrying that you'll be an incompetent leader. They must trust your judgment, temperament, and ability to "TCB"—that's right, take care of business!

Frankly, basic integrity principles are lacking in the current day business world (not to mention in the political arena), and that scares leaders. They want to surround themselves with good people who they know can contribute to a successful team, but these people can be hard to find. When you're a key member of a team, your leaders want to trust that you'll get the job done so they can relax and focus on other aspects of their duties. If they are able to concentrate on more macro elements, such as developing new client relationships, while you handle everyday micro elements, such as meeting deadlines, your team and overall organization will be more effective.

The cost, time, and effort of monitoring the basic tasks of an employee is quite high, and rarely do people actually enjoy being micro-managers, because it takes talented leaders' minds and efforts off thinking about strategic tasks and bigger opportunities. Therefore having employees whose ethics and reliability are unquestionable is of serious value to both the leader and the organization.

MIND SWITCH FACT

In February 2015, Bloomberg surveyed recruiters in 547 companies regarding hiring of MBAs. In all industries—chemical, consulting, consumer, energy, finance, healthcare, manufacturing, pharmaceuticals, retail, technology, and transportation—one of the least common and most desired skills across all industries was leadership.

The popular buzzword "transparency" is bandied about a lot more than it's actually put into practice, but being transparent with your boss, manager, or director is important. They'll not only respect you more, but they'll know they can trust you to tell the truth and act accordingly. And that's imperative—keep in mind, as a "follower," you are integral to the success of your leaders. Leaders realize they are likely to get "played" sometimes, whether by the government, customers or vendors, direct reports or bosses, and more. If they can consistently rely on you to support them—not to lie to, steal from, or cheat and swindle them—you will stand out.

Proving you are trustworthy takes time. Effective leaders have every right, and the definite need, to test their team to see what they are made of. Therefore the smallest transgressions get noticed. As a follower, leaving even the tiniest question about your trustworthiness will start closing the door a little at a time for future stretch assignments and growth opportunities. If leaders trust you, however, they will take a chance on you, and as you help them succeed, they will help you in turn. That being said, just because they feel they can trust you does not necessarily mean you're on the path to leadership—other traits, including self-confidence, play a major role.

Self-Confident, *Not* Arrogant

In general, people will accept you as you first present yourself until they have evidence that proves you aren't what you seem. It may be a cliché, but first impressions are crucial. Nowhere is this more important than when you meet someone at your organization, or in your industry, who is in a position of power above you—for example a CEO, middle manager, or other leader. If you display a sense of confidence when meeting and interacting with leaders for the first time, they will not only remember you, but they are likely to have an immediate sense of confidence in you. If you are arrogant, act self-important, or have an egotistical attitude, you will certainly not be forgotten either—but for the wrong reasons.

Just as leaders are kindly confident, as outlined in Chapter 2, followers aspiring to leadership roles must exude confidence as well. Confidence is two pronged. First and foremost, it is what you feel *inside*. Second, it is what you show the world externally. Inner self-confidence comes from your attitude and accomplishments, whereas external confidence comes from self-discipline, practice, and the ability to express your genuine self.

To develop internal confidence, you need to seek success, even when it comes to small tasks. Over time, these smaller successes will add up, increasing your confidence to take on larger endeavors. Begin by doing something tangible that you know you can do well. For example, if your company is disorganized about meeting follow-up (like many companies) and you are a great synthesizer of information, then use that gap in company capability as an opening for you to shine. After meetings you attend, send a brief and courteous capture of the highlights and to-dos. Offer to schedule a follow-up instead of waiting. Then try to achieve two more successes of growing importance in that same arena. In our experience, it takes three favorable outcomes to make you start believing you can perform better in a particular area. True inner confidence comes from that deliberate exercise leading to progressively more difficult situations. If you are the great synthesizer we talked about earlier, before long you

> "Don't make me have to hold your hand. I don't have time to give constant approval. I will as much as I can, but showing you don't need it every step of the way shows me your self-confidence."

will be sitting in on increasingly important meetings with more senior folks because you will have shown yourself to be thoughtful and succinct. As one CEO friend of Debra's says, "The first time you succeed you think 'man, was I lucky.' The second time you think, 'Wow, lightning struck twice, I guess.' The third time you finally own it, 'Yes, it was due to me.'"

After you have created a string of small successes, start collecting the evidence of your accomplishments. If you increase the speed of a task by being more organized (as with the meeting example), or save money or drive revenue because you took initiative where others didn't, do your best to quantify those outcomes immediately after they occur and share them with others. If others agree that your contribution changed the outcome, you will have evidence and perspective you didn't have before. You'll learn a lot about yourself and better understand the kind of problems you are attracted to, what approach you use to deal with them, and the results. Remember, as a leader or a follower, your impact is evidence.

> "Be tenacious and persistent. You'll surprise yourself with what you can do if you don't give up."

Building self-awareness is part of your tenacious pursuit of results and will increase your inner confidence. As you examine your successes, think about what you can do differently next time for even better results. This process takes competence and a willingness to constantly learn, so you must be vigilant. If you are, you'll find yourself mastering skills, trades, and processes that will then further boost your inner confidence. Then, it's time to work on your external confidence!

Developing external confidence also takes time and sincere effort. Many people find it difficult to display their confidence, as they worry about coming across as egotistical or self-involved. If you've done good, valuable work, however, you should be comfortable in your success. Don't let yourself think your accomplishments are "no big deal"—be proud of your contributions that have made a difference and talk about those experiences openly (just don't brag about them!). The way you communicate and express yourself will be noted time and again by your bosses and managers.

An outside show of confidence requires physical discipline and a serene demeanor. Stand up straight, not hunched over like you're typing on a computer. Maintain a calm voice and a relaxed smile so you look approachable, competent, and confident: scared people have a blank face, while confident people smile. Speak slowly—if you're talking quickly, you will seem nervous, and when you seem nervous you cause other people to be nervous (because they begin wondering what you are so nervous about!)

> **"Don't be arrogant with me, the customers, your subordinates, vendors, or anyone you come in contact with. It's the surest sign of lacking confidence."**

Another step to developing external confidence is by consistently considering the positive, productive, and constructive side of your life and work. Shut out negative, unproductive, and destructive distractions. You don't have to entirely ignore the bad side—you're likely to lose your mind that way—but you should put more energy into the upside. One way to do this is by avoiding negative people. This will help you create a positive attitude, even an energy, that others will recognize and respond to. It can be tough, but it's worth the effort.

Keep in mind that you want to seem confident, not entitled. You want to show that you believe you deserve the opportunity to take on more responsibilities and, over time, enter a leadership role. People have the tendency, however, to acquire an inflated sense of self-worth, many times through parents, or other influential individuals early in their lives, who pump them up with an overabundant self-esteem.

Sonia Cheng, the millennial CEO of Rosewood Hotel Group, certainly has a lot to be confident about. By the age of 29 she had already begun overseeing the international hotel chain, which has 55 hotels across 18 countries. Instead of having an inflated ego, however, she remains humble amid her success. "Perhaps the most important lesson I've learned," she told us, "is that no matter how successful you may become, do not fall victim to ego and pride, and it's always through humility that you really open your eyes to how the world is changing."

> "Refrain from trying to show how smart you are to me or anyone else. I know you are. I am interested in your thinking, so tell me. Tell me how you see the problem, what you want to do about it, and what you hope to achieve from it. That shows confidence."

Make sure you keep your ego in check—there are already enough self-entitled jerks out there, and you don't want to join their ranks. Stick with a positive attitude, which will open up conversation and a general good-naturedness. It will also make you more desirable to be around.

Easy to Be Around

People in leadership roles have the latitude to decide whom they want to hang with. That's one of the perks. If you're a pain in the whatever, they will not want to spend time with you. Sure, some employees may want to avoid their bosses like the plague, but if you're looking toward the future and have aspirations to lead your own team or business one day, both your boss and peers have to enjoy your company.

One way to make sure you're not the office pariah is by being able and willing to laugh at yourself. Be happy when people kid around with you at work; that means they see promise in you. They don't bother ribbing the employees that they don't support. Good up-and-coming leaders see the humor in the unpredictability of their jobs and lives in general. Without that ability, you won't be able to handle a leadership role in the future. We promise you, no matter the amount of stress you're under now, when you're the head honcho of a multimillion- or multibillion-dollar company, or when you have to answer to shareholders, or when people depend on you so they can put food on their tables at home, you will be entering a whole new world of concern. A sense of humor will get you much further than you may ever know: it's no coincidence that there is a similarity between the words "funny bone" and "backbone."

"Don't be easily offended. If you make me walk on eggshells around you, I won't bother. If something that I do seriously offends you, take me aside, and with a calm tone of voice ask, 'What was going on with your comment about . . . ?' Your confidence in bringing it up to me will generate respect."

In addition to having a good sense of humor, leaders need to know that you'll simply be easy to work with. Otherwise, why would they want you on their teams? With so many choices open to leaders today in regard to potential employees—remote workers, global workers, robots—they don't need to waste their time with people who require more

> **"Get a reputation as a game changer who makes a positive difference in other people's lives. If you're not having fun at my company, you are doing it wrong."**

attention than they are willing to or able to provide. If you are easy to instruct and they can delegate work to you without hassle, then they will. If you make it difficult for them, they won't. There is always someone else waiting in the wings that they can bring onto their team. Recent research shows young people tend to want to stay with a company no more than two to three years—well, trust me, a leader who finds you difficult to work with will not wait for two to three years to get rid of you.

Leaders also want employees who aren't going to whine or complain all the time. They want employees who understand that they are there to do a job, so no matter the circumstances, they have to suck it up and do it. It's okay to tell a boss or other leader, "I want to make sure I know all I can at this point to make this happen," but annoying her or him with unnecessary questions, or requiring constant attention, will not help you in any way. You're likely to not receive the answers you're looking for, and, in the meantime, you come across as needy and clueless.

> **"Never feel something is beneath you. It isn't. If it's something that has to be done, do it."**

Lastly, and most simply, be nice! People remember how you treat them for a long time—if you're rude, insulting, or unwelcoming, they won't forget. If you alienate the people around you, you miss out on important opportunities that will help you on your path to leadership. Even something simple like remembering a person's name helps build your reputation as being amiable and congenial. Stewart Butterfield, cofounder of Slack and Flickr, may have put it best when he said in *Business Insider* (*The CEO of $3.8 Billion Slack Has a Smart Idea to Help People Get off Work Early*, August 2016), "Work hard and be good to other people or you won't have the life you want to have."

The Mind Switch on Being a Good Follower

To get good followers, you have to be a great leader. To be a great leader, you had to be a good follower at some point to learn important lessons that contribute to a team's or company's success. No matter how high you go up an organization, you need support from below, as well as receptivity from above. Of all the expected traits, the most important are a strong work ethic to show you have the right stuff; the ability to engage with questions instead of a know-it-all pontification; the confidence to accomplish goals, and get others to have confidence in you; and a demeanor that is easy to be around.

> "Do whatever is asked of you even if you don't want to or know why. That will earn you the right to ask why."

The most important aspect to being a good follower, however, is being a person who is trustworthy. All else is close to worthless if your leaders, team members, colleagues, or customers are unable to trust you. The mind switch requires a deep and clear understanding that you cannot hide a lack of integrity. It will be posted, tweeted, blogged, and go viral quickly and be nearly impossible to rectify. Nothing that is expected of you as a follower is less than you'd demand in a person that *you* decide to follow. Being a good follower will open the door to your own future leadership role.

STORIES FROM THE ROAD

Jose Zavala, system analyst in supply chain at Starbucks, supporting Latin America, writes about differentiating yourself with leaders.

In the fall of 2010, I found myself, like many college kids, preparing for a career fair in order to find an internship/job after graduation. The job search process looked hard and was a time-consuming task. Most college students prepared a résumé, rehearsed the answers to the basic questions asked in interviews—for example, "Tell me about you?" and "Why should I hire you?"—printed 100 résumés, and gave them to as many people as possible. The conversations with recruiters were quick and mostly about the résumé—there was not too much time to build rapport or a relationship with the interviewers.

If students landed an interview, they brought their best acting skills and rehearsed their best speech they had been memorizing for the interview. I felt that in this process, recruiters were filtering by the tangible measurements (GPA, examples of leadership, experience, etc.), and most of the kids were selling the same skills. There was nothing interesting or different about this process. I thought to myself, how can you differentiate and have the companies look for you and not you for them?

I felt that students did not have much leverage and their goal was just to land a job, not the best job, and the best jobs are not found in the universities' career fairs. The point here is that just by observing, I found a niche/gap that I could use to make this process better and more fun for my job search.

I spent time studying the job market to be a better player. The first thing I did was ask myself, if I was a senior executive in my field, what would I be doing with my free time? What would I be reading? And who would I be hanging out with?

I would google local companies, find their executive names, and through LinkedIn or companies' websites (where they have executives' biographies), I would look at what associations they belong to.

I am in the field of supply chain, and by doing some searches I subscribed to the same magazines these executives subscribed to and also read them. I found that there were breakfasts/networking events in my city where senior leaders in my field get together to network, to get insights about the industry and talk about other cool stuff!

I reached out and asked if I could attend (I told a compelling story and I mentioned that I was a student). As soon as you say "student," people love it! People love to help students and especially if you come from their alma mater.

At the same time I would cold call people, or as I read interesting articles on the Internet I would e-mail the author of the article. Failure rate is high and most people will not respond, but if you use key words like "student" and "learn" you can build rapport with people.

The most important thing I learned was to give these famous authors/executives a perspective. Find something interesting and send it to them. This way you become a resource and an interesting guy. My goal was to help them be smarter. Doing this, people start having an interest in you, and I found this approach to be the best way to have access to the best jobs! The best jobs for students are not posted on their school's career website. You need to be book smart (meaning having the tangibles companies look for), but also a degree of street smart where you find ways to create choices and have leaders and companies look for you.

〈〈〈〉〉〉

Eliza Cross, president of Cross Media, which helps businesses and professionals develop strategic marketing solutions, distinctive brands, and effective, memorable communications, writes about showing up.

My former business partner Pat Wiesner and I volunteered to mentor a high school class in one of Denver's poorest neighborhoods. Week after week we visited the classroom and tried to break through the barriers, but the students talked, laughed, pushed chairs around, and mostly ignored us.

Pat and I brainstormed, and wondered if getting the kids away from school might change the dynamics. We proposed a field trip to our publishing company, persuaded the teacher, requested a school bus, and got permission slips returned. We printed T-shirts for all the kids, ordered a catered lunch, and planned activities that we hoped would be fun and engaging.

On the day of the field trip, the school bus pulled up and exactly two boys stepped out. All of the other students had ditched that day.

We were deeply disappointed, and we also had the challenge of what to do for the pair who had shown up. After a quiet company tour, we ate our enormous meal and tried to make awkward conversation. That's when Pat and I decided to change our plans.

After lunch, we took the boys over to nearby Centennial Airport so they could see our company's King Air. They were pretty impressed with the airplane, and even climbed into the cockpit. We took photos, they smiled, and things started to thaw. I stopped at the bank on my way back to the office.

We regrouped in the conference room with our two protégés, and I held up two envelopes. "Pat and I are very proud of you two for showing up today," I said. "Everyone else ditched, but not you. Because you two made the effort, we have something to give you." I handed each boy an envelope.

Peeking inside, they each discovered $100 in cash. One of the boys looked like he was going to cry. "Are you serious?" he whispered.

"It's yours; you earned it," Pat said. "The lesson we hope you take away from today is this: If you don't show up, nothing will happen. But if you *show up*, something great might happen. We hope you keep showing up."

05

THE UPS AND DOWNS OF BEING A LEADER

erhaps you are a rising star—exhibiting the qualities discussed in Chapter 4—and the people around you recognize your potential. Or maybe you are a midcareer professional whose peers and managers tend to push you into unchartered waters often, ones that you are trying to learn to navigate. Or it's possible that you are an experienced leader, having conquered your role within a company or enterprise. No matter what stage of your career, if you are a business leader, or looking to become one, you probably have a list of reasons why you've chosen this path. Some are nobler than others, let's say, making a difference in the world versus making a whole lot of loot, but no matter your motivation, it's easy to sometimes lose sight of what's important.

Let's face it, being a leader isn't just roses and accolades all the time. Every leadership journey has bumps in the road due to circumstances both within and out of your control. For example, as humans we are prone to paranoia. It is natural to have moments of uncertainty and confusion throughout your career, where the steps are not as clear as you'd like them to be. You'll experience stress, anxiety, and mounting pressures that will make you want to throw in the towel and give up on your aspirations. The leadership mind switch, however, is here to help clarify the qualities and motivations that will keep propelling you forward.

This chapter is to remind you why you should stay on the path that you mapped out when you first felt the gravitational pull toward a leadership role. We want you to remember that leadership is fulfilling, fun, and, simply put, cool. Not only do we want to talk about the benefits of being a leader, but we also want to comment on some of the challenges and downsides. Trust us, however, the good certainly outweighs the bad.

The Freedom of Leadership

Being a leader is a lot better than being the sidekick. Yes, the world needs both, but if you're as smart, ambitious, techno-logically adept, socially conscious, personally responsible, and growth-oriented as others running the show, why not step up and be more accountable for the results? The freedom that comes with the responsibility can be exhilarating, and that adrenalin will help you survive, focus, and ultimately perform at a higher level.

This freedom includes the opportunity to have more control over your own work and actions. We of course have never heard people in a professional setting say they like *less* control over their activities, but the nuance of how this happens is sometimes contrary to expectation. The very concept of leadership includes the ability to leverage your skills by mobilizing others toward a goal. You spend less time "in the trenches," and, in return, get to focus more on desired results. However, you end up working hardest during the most intense periods, where stress is high and decisions are crucial.

Luckily, as a leader you also have more support. For example, if you are in a role where you have an assistant, you can manage your calendar better than before. This creates greater flexibility. You will then often initiate, instead of accept, meetings and set schedules based around your availability and time frame. Such flexibility also gives you the opportunity to concentrate on what you see as priorities and allows you to lobby for, and make, changes when necessary to succeed.

Following others can be grueling at times—you may or may not agree with the way your boss wants things done on any given day. You may think a different strategy would be more successful or a different market more lucrative. If you are passionate about what you do, disagreements are inevitable, but the reality of the situation is that *observing* is a lot easier than *doing*. It is easier to criticize and edit from the sidelines than it is to be the one who is on the hook for a whole team's, organization's, or movement's results. I would challenge you to honestly state that you have never complained about being forced to comply with some management mandate, following some process that seems to be from the dark ages, or meeting some impossible goal set for you.

As a leader, however, you're the one who sets the goals. You can identify processes and activities that don't make sense to you and reinvent a more appealing path to whatever results you are aiming for. For example, you can alter that meeting structure that you have always questioned, reorganize the team for higher productivity, or completely revamp the way your business creates, sells, and delivers products and services. In essence, you get to minimize processes, actions, and assumptions that *you* think are stupid. Of course, this also means that you have to put the proverbial "money where your mouth is," so make sure you develop a good radar about the "stupidity" of one thing or another before making sweeping assumptions.

In addition to setting the goals, you have more authority to take action on achieving them. Your team members will recognize this fact, which will allow for faster movement toward success. Natural leaders are forward-leaning in their approach, they are not passive observers. They gain the respect and trust of others by being able to make decisions, prioritize, and gain consensus needed to progress causes, businesses, and even communities. With the confidence of their team behind them, they avoid self-doubt and maintain a high level of kindly confidence. Such an attitude will also help them in dealing with the typical bureaucracy of any organization. Of course the level of bureaucracy varies dramatically across workplaces, and may still be a limiting factor, but leaders will find ways to reduce the bottlenecks within their control to help them successfully execute. This means less frustration, more potential to outmaneuver competitors, and a greater ability to focus on the long term.

With these freedoms, however, you won't always know exactly what to do. Until you are tested in a very wide range of scenarios, it can be difficult to understand how you will approach specific situations, especially riskier ones that may have uncertain outcomes. It is even harder to know how others will respond to them. Risk tolerance is a very personal thing, yet when you are part of a team, you are captive to the judgments of others. Whether you are launching a product, selling in a new way, restructuring a department, or creating a new service, you will have to make critical choices. As the head of a team, though, it's up to you decide what chances are worth taking. The faster you can navigate your way into leading initiatives, projects, and ultimately organizations, the closer you get to that opportunity. This prospect can be a scary one, but it's also incredibly exciting.

In many ways, your freedom as a leader relies greatly on your team and the other people you surround yourself with. In turn, as a leader, you get to decide who those people are. It is almost needless to say that who you work with matters—a lot. The Bureau of Labor Statistics states that typical employees in the United States work an average of 7.8 hours a day. If you are in a thriving industry, company, or organization, you may work more hours, and if you are in a turnaround situation, where there has been bad performance that needs to be rectified, you probably work way more than this. By extension, professionals that have to commute, utilize work-related devices when not in the office, and travel regularly probably spend, at most, five to six waking hours with their loved ones or at leisure—much less than their time with colleagues. The point is that you'd better like the folks you work with because you will see them, socialize with them, and interact with them more than almost anyone else in your life. Yet so many people are forced to tolerate subpar colleagues or peers because they don't take the next step toward leading something significant.

MIND SWITCH FACT

In 2015, The Organisation for Economic Co-operation and Development (OECD) determined the workweek for countries:

Hours
United States: 34.40
Australia: 32.00
Mexico: 42.85
Japan: 33.25
France: 28.33
Germany: 26.37

Choosing the people around you doesn't mean that you should pursue friendships over competence in the workplace. However, the better leader you are, the more choices you have when it comes to selecting your direct reports. You can also choose the people around you by *only* pursuing opportunities to work with individuals or teams that inspire you. On your leadership journey, there will be times when you have to take assignments that are painful because of the people involved. These assignments, however, are a gift as they provide important lessons and the motivation to never have to do them, with those people, again!

The Ability to Make an Impact

In addition to the freedom awarded by a leadership role, leaders also have the unique opportunity to directly impact the world around them. History tells us that humans are drawn to progress and frustrated by inertia. The authority to produce results is a privilege, one that drives ordinary people to become extraordinary. Unforgettable leaders make huge sacrifices in their personal lives in the spirit of progress and success. Those that have been able to turn around economies, create and save jobs, end wars, and mediate tragic situations will be remembered and revered long after they are gone.

Leadership provides the stage to create magic in whatever domain you have chosen. While "impact" is a subjective concept, strong leaders seek paths that open the most doors and influence results—they deliver not only on their own dreams but also on those of their team and the people who use their products or services. This lasting impact comes from the difficult decisions they must make every single day. The process of decision making, however, has changed over time, especially with the technological advances of the fourth industrial revolution, where algorithms and artificial intelligence are a part of everyday life.

MIND SWITCH FACT

In July 2016, Michael Kassner wrote in the *Tech Republic* (*Decision-Making Algorithms: Is Anyone Making Sure They're Right?*) that algorithms are used to make decisions in:

» Search engine personalization
» Criminal risk of recidivism
» Advertising systems
» Employee evaluations
» Banking/finance
» Political campaigns

Decision making has become easier in some ways, but harder in others due to society's progressing capabilities to create data and use it intelligently. Today, people have access to better algorithms and other tools to assess the way their customers, constituents, and audience react to the things they sell, say, or implement. We have machines to analyze feedback and even forecast future trends. With these mountains of data, however, it can be difficult to decide what's important and how it can positively affect your team, company, and you, if at all. As a leader, you need to be able to rely on the "human elements"—instinct, experience, and creativity—to make the best decisions possible. Still, sometimes you won't know if you've made the right ones.

"Being right" in a decision you have made is a question of perspective and history. At the time you make a decision, you never actually know whether tomorrow you will regret it or celebrate it. That said, as a leader, you get to decide what *you* believe is right and then follow through with the appropriate action. This means leaning on values to make a final choice about what to do in a situation. When it comes to a values-based decision, you may find yourself at odds with your company or team. Every organization has values irrespective of whether they are explicit or implied by the behavior of its people. The best companies have values that are consistently applied and reflect the culture accurately. However, sometimes that culture needs to change, or get back on track, and if you're a leader within that organization, you have the opportunity to facilitate that change. Doing what you think is right can be a powerful driver. The effective leaders we've spoken with have told us that some of the most rewarding and impactful actions they've taken have been simple expressions of their values. Of course, if you are a leader only in name and don't hold influence over others, then you'll never get anything accomplished.

Being able to influence with grace is one of the top demarcation lines between managers and leaders. Managers allocate resources and provide direction, while leaders achieve results and inspire action based on their ability to directly and indirectly influence outcomes. Chief strategists, presidents, chief security officers, and many other executive level positions rely heavily on influencing others. It takes an adept mind and nimble communication skills to master the art of influence—simply reading Robert Cialdini's books on the topic won't get you there.

Rising leaders generally master influencing down (over employees) more quickly than up (bosses and managers) or across (direct peers or colleagues). But being able to get results by tactfully giving the directions you want followed to those that are best placed to make things happen is a key skill irrespective of whether you need someone more senior, junior, or equal to you to do it. The harsh reality is that it is far easier for rising leaders, those who are still learning the ropes, to get the people who work for them to follow directions. The next, much harder, step is influencing up. The concept of influencing up is pivotal to great leadership because if you are going to make change happen or forge new initiatives, you need those ahead of you in the hierarchy to appreciate and enable your activities and support them explicitly. This skill takes some mastery and a deft touch at times; it takes

> "I am working on developing my 'commanding' leadership style. I really value collaborating and motivating my colleagues toward a common goal. That said, sometimes it is just necessary to get sh*% done."

emotional intelligence to understand how direct or nuanced you need to be in asking for things and informing those who need to know about your objectives to be able to support you.

Influencing across and "out" can also be difficult and downright hazardous at times. It is not uncommon for rising leaders, and even nimble masters, to stumble in this area. Sometimes you will find yourself in a situation where you have a healthy working relationship with a peer that becomes as prickly as a cactus overnight when the pressure turns on and you need to apply your influence. Rubbing up against a relationship that was fine until you need to collaborate, compete, or delegate can be confusing the first time. But you should always welcome it as an opportunity to grow and learn how to work with others to create the utmost impact.

When you first become a leader, it can be daunting to decide on the impact you plan to have. Sometimes you come across opportunities that you would never have been able to forecast. This is the case for most leaders we know: they set out on a path, had the right mindset for leadership, took chances that others didn't, and followed their desire to do more with their life. They weren't daunted by failure along the way and knew that even a small step in the right direction to being a significant leader would be rewarding. They found that they could make a major impact and, in doing so, they ended up building their own legacy.

The Opportunity to Build a Legacy

Being remembered for the impact you have made and the positive things you have done is a basic human desire. Reading about the people and companies that you helped propel forward and receiving thank you notes decades later for the way you changed people's outlooks or influenced their careers is immeasurably fulfilling. In the era we currently live in, we would be forgiven for thinking that Twitter followers, shares on LinkedIn, Facebook likes, Snapchat friends, and Qora responses are a measure of our success as a person and in our professional lives.

These social media channels are all fun ways to build an audience for your activities, develop skills in generating content, and share your thoughts on issues or ideas that matter to you. They are no substitute, however, for being able to see the real impact of your contributions. Yes, fourth generation leaders must utilize all the relevant tools available to them, but their tangible results—the products they create, the markets they conquer, the other leaders they nurture—will be their lasting legacy. If you start a company that employs others, then you help boost the economy. If you master a skill, you can use it in the future for the good of not only your office or community, but the entire world—your day job does not need be in the social sector or clearly in the line of humanitarian causes for you to have an everlasting impact.

Leaders have the opportunity to build something greater than themselves through an ongoing process of growth and influence. It's important for them to think and act in the long term, even when they need to make short-term decisions. As they learn more, they utilize their knowledge and expertise, and then pass it along to others, either

> **"The kindest feedback I have ever had in my career is when a team member once said to me, 'I would follow you into a fire.'"**

formally, as a coach for example, or informally as a mentor. Leading others gives you a channel for sharing your wisdom and directing energy toward people who contribute the most to your company, organization, or cause.

As a mentor, your mentees will remember you forever, and your investment in their development will play out in unexpected and unknown ways. For example, a South African immigrant student read Debra's first book, *Lions Don't Need to Roar*, and contacted her. He explained he was new to the United States and to the working world, but he found her book incredibly helpful. He asked if he could speak with her periodically as he started his career, and Debra happily agreed. Over time they lost contact until one day Debra received an invite to attend a meeting with the ambassador of South Africa—it turned out the student had returned to his home country and was now the chief of staff! He remembered his first American mentor. Many of Debra's young mentees whom she met as "pups" grew up to be "big dogs" and have since surprised her with invitations to events and assignments in foreign countries as the mentees grew into positions of power and influence.

The number of people you mentor is not constrained by an org chart or official reporting system. It is only constrained by your time and desire to help other people grow. Also, for you rising leaders, keep in mind that you don't need to be "older" to become a mentor—you have particular knowledge and skills that members of all generations could likely benefit from. This idea is typically referred to as "reverse mentoring."

When Debra started her career she relied heavily on mentors to help her learn what she wanted and has continued that practice to this day. She has over 100 people she can call and talk to about any issue when she wants another experienced point of view or different perspective. The problem, however, is that many of her mentors are, or were, older, which means some have died, some have Alzheimer's, and one is even in prison. A number of years back she decided to continue to learn from others who have knowledge she needed that was largely in the digital and virtual arena, and she realized she'd have to get young mentors. The exchange has been an excellent experience in which she gives them the information and insight they seek from her years of experience and they show her how to Snapchat. Debra will never forget these "give-and-take" relationships, nor are her mentors and mentees likely to forget her anytime soon.

Of course, one of the issues with mentoring is the time. Who has spare hours to dedicate to something with a long-term payoff? Good leaders will prioritize mentoring and reverse mentoring because they are enlightened and know it is part of the gig. Being generous to those who give their time to you will ensure that future asks are not a burden. A favorite technique of Debra's is to purchase two of any new technology and give one to her young tech mentor and keep one for herself. As the tech mentor learns, she or he simultaneously teaches Debra, which measurably decreases the learning curve for Debra.

These types of mentoring experiences result in leaders gaining new followers, people who look up to them and aspire to their greatness. Even more rewarding, however, is the leader's experience in helping to create and develop future leaders. It is a common leadership meme that you should surround yourself with people who are better than you and hire with a view to replacing yourself in the future. The ability to identify and develop that potential is imperative. It takes a self-confident and enlightened leader to hire talented team members and help them succeed. It is your job to fight through any temptation to staff only for the present or be suspicious of candidates that seem overly ambitious—making leaders, those that someday may end up with your job, takes guts.

It may be emotionally difficult to hire those people who will potentially replace you in the future, but it is simply part of being a good leader. It is probably no coincidence that the first half of the word *succession* is "success," yet this element of leadership—succession planning—can be a sensitive one. The good news is that the demand for leaders is such that making more of them will benefit you now and later, and when all is said and done, they, too, will become part of your legacy. As Mahatma Gandhi once wrote, "A sign of a good leader is not how many followers you have, but how many leaders you create." Not only is the creation of leaders necessary for progress, for the existence of humanity, even, but it is also the ultimate legacy.

Leadership Downsides

There is a cost of living your life as a leader. If it was easy, everyone would do it. The realization that leading is both difficult and hard work will happen early in your journey. It will likely result in you eating some humble pie and having more respect for your predecessors or peers or team members. There will be instances where you step into a leadership role in a company in which the historical, cultural, or technical context for why things have been done a certain way for years is not clear—up will be down and down will be up.

More generally, however, you'll likely end up feeling isolated at times—as the saying goes, it's "lonely at the top."

Your employees may have a strong relationship with one another but end up seeing you as the enemy, the "bad guy," or simply separate from the team. They'll find you intimidating, knowing that you can potentially make or break their careers, which will lead to a lack of transparency and goodwill. They'll be extra careful about what they say around you and routinely check for your approval, feeling out your intentions and motivations. You will be suspect until they really trust you.

Even after you gain your employees' trust, you still need to worry about the affect your actions and decisions have on them, those above you, and the rest of the business. You will be blamed for failures, whether real or perceived, that you didn't necessarily have control over. Even if it isn't your fault, you'll take the heat for any mistake made under your watch. If you make a bad choice and are blind to the ramifications, you'll end up on the hot seat. You'll be under constant scrutiny as people watch and analyze your every move. Most people will focus on the negatives and overlook your commitment, relentless effort, long working hours, massive amounts of responsibility, and your risk-taking attitude—all the things that got you into a leadership position in the first place.

As long as you truly want to make a positive impact on your world, however, these problems are all surmountable. As we highlighted in Chapters 02 and 03, good fourth generation leaders are tenacious and enlightened—they don't shy away from problems, they run toward them. You have to be willing to put some muscle, sweat, and intellect into the process—being a great leader requires work and responsibility. Ultimately, if you take your job and role seriously enough, the rewards of leadership will outweigh the costs.

Mind Switch on the Benefits of Leadership

While this chapter is technically about the ups and downs of leadership, we are definite believers in the simple fact that being a leader is cool, and we think you should go for it! The freedoms that decision-making positions provide are a privilege and allow you to make thoughtful choices in who you work with and how you spend your time. Creating an impact is the role of a leader, but the magnitude of the impact is up to you. You can dial it up or down, fulfill your dreams, or simply hit the set goals. All are valuable, but the ability to choose that path is highly rewarding.

One of your greatest opportunities as a successful leader is to make more leaders. You can mentor. You can coach. You can change lives. And in the process, you will leave a legacy that will reflect your values and your beliefs. On the flip side, leading is a huge responsibility and can be isolating. In the new world of work it will be more demanding than it has ever been. The cocktail of generations and styles that you will interact with every day as your team, peers, and bosses become more diverse will be unlike any you have ever seen. Mistakes will be uncovered and surfaced faster than ever, and wins will be expected, not celebrated, as there is always a disruptive competitor around the corner. But the main reward is still as beautiful as ever: an opportunity to express yourself and build an enduring trail of your professional existence that others carry forward into the future.

STORIES FROM THE ROAD

**Dean Campos, founder of Clear Legend LLC,
a talent company that helps people find millennial
talent, writes about becoming a rising leader.**

We are living in a very exciting time within a digital age not only from a business perspective, but in also dealing with personnel. Competitive companies are seeking highly qualified talent to be the next developed generation of future business leaders. While working for several different companies within operations as a millennial, I have observed this challenge consistently for years, and it is continuing to worsen.

This issue arose specifically in my career because of senior leaders and midlevel millennial mangers not being able to connect with one another. This not only led to a lack of communication by both parties, but also this disconnect affected team culture drastically, which had a direct correlation to performance and overall retention.

The common perception I have observed with senior leadership in regard to millennials entering the workforce is that they are not "like them" in thought processes and attitudes toward business. This is slowly becoming a bigger and bigger problem within many different organizations. Soon this problem will be so impactful companies will feel the pressure from a financial, culture, and retention perspective, being unable to drive performance. The reality is there are millennial leaders who want the same things as seasoned senior leaders. There is just a relational disconnect.

This disconnect is presented in the understanding of people specifically in generational knowledge, ability to identify core values, a leader's capability in leveraging the strengths of senior leadership, and being able to balance a culture of positivity. These core principles of relational excellence exist, but only in highly talented individuals.

We have found millennials who possess this skill set to not only be important, but vital to the successful operation of any organization. The transition is already happening in businesses, and the challenge is small now, but will become an even bigger problem as we move forward going into the next five years. We recruit these highly talented professionals and deem them "Millennial Hybrids." They are highly skilled and posses a level of relational excellence that cannot be taught. The complex nature of assessing candidates at their core makes the recruiting process crucial to business survival and its ability to thrive.

We at Clear Legend have a dedicated team of millennial hybrids able to identify the next generation of leaders who encompass relational excellence. We create value by seeking millennial hybrids who understand the vital importance of team cohesion while expressing a common language bridging the gaps between different generations in business.

PART TWO

Management, Leadership, or Both?

Knowing how to hire, understanding the traits that matter the most to you, and realizing how good and bad hiring impacts your success, are all crucial to being a good leader.

Much has been written about the dividing line between management and leadership. We think there is value in a conversation about the differences between the two—especially for those trying to make the jump from management to leadership—but we also think the debate has been overdone. The reason for this view is that the distinction can be portrayed as relatively clear-cut in academic and theoretical articles on the topic, almost as if we choose one path or the other. In reality we are all on a spectrum of mastering the skills needed to be both a manager and leader, so it is not a choice that people make, it is a journey that can take a lifetime.

Good managers and good leaders equally need character and ability, while exhibiting the behaviors and attitudes we discussed throughout Part One. Our experience is that good leaders rarely start as bad managers. We believe leadership is the higher order goal, but the traits required to be a good leader must be developed and mastered in tandem with the day-to-day tasks of management. Some leaders are just born with the ability to do both, but the majority of great leaders got to their positions through practice, consideration, reflection, feedback, success, and failure.

As mentioned earlier in the book, managing is largely about allocating resources and the tactical handling of operations, while leading is about the higher order aspiration of bringing others along with you toward a common goal. The practice of managing and overseeing others' work often provides the experience required to be a credible leader for the future. It also develops important traits, like empathy, and technical skills that you can't easily acquire without having done the work.

The traits, behaviors, and skills that make you a successful manager will also make you a good leader. That said, not all good managers will be able to make the leadership transition. In our experience, those who struggle with seeing the big picture and building strong relationships do not make great leadership material. They get caught in the minutia and don't invest in building alliances within their organization. This section provides you with the building blocks to improve in these two areas and thrive in the new world of work

The evolution from manager to leader happens when you are able to:

1. Teach and inspire others to accomplish shared goals
2. Identify and recognize gaps in your own knowledge
3. Build a team around you to conquer new challenges

The very best leaders can do all three at scale, consistently, and at the required speed.

The topics discussed in this part of the book (Part Two) are those that your future mentees will likely ask you about. Good leaders will be able to articulate their views on each topic with storytelling and examples, passion, and experience. It is not enough just to know how to do things required in leadership, you need to be able to share and teach them to others also. We have structured this section of the book to be picked up and read topic by topic whenever you need to. These topics are evergreen, and being prepared to handle each of them skillfully within the setting of the speed and disruption of the fourth revolution will serve you well throughout your leadership journey.

BASIC LEADERSHIP RESPONSIBILITIES

06

Even the most seemingly simple management and leadership responsibilities can become incredibly complicated if not approached correctly. In fact, the "basics" aren't necessarily basic at all when you are the one that has to execute on them. Knowing and doing are two very different things. Learning how to handle sensitive issues like giving hard feedback or making someone's role redundant takes time and effort. Further, as a manager, everything you do counts in a way that you might not have expected despite your experience—others are watching your every move for clues and signals for what is to come. This chapter focuses on four essential tasks that leaders deal with on a consistent basis: hiring employees, letting employees go, providing (or denying) time off, and hosting meetings. Let's begin by looking at one of the most essential of these leadership responsibilities—hiring great talent.

Hiring Employees

As a leader, hiring employees is one of the hardest things you have to do. The process can be grueling and mistakes are possible: you are working with imperfect information, taking risks on company culture integration, and weighing opportunity costs in every situation. Opportunity costs arise because once a position is filled, hiring managers can't easily change their minds. Even if they suddenly decide that a different profile was needed for that role, or that a different position should have been a higher priority, they need to be accountable for their decisions and move forward.

As leaders develop within an enterprise, there is a point where their ability to build their own team, as opposed to inheriting teams from others, will determine their success. And how you go about hiring can depend on the business cycle you are in or the type of company. If you are in a growth business, for example, where annual rates of expansion are higher than average for your industry, or you are in a young company, then hiring is all about finding people who are not only result-oriented, but oriented toward outcomes that can unlock even further gains in the future (as opposed to maintaining the status quo). These people must also have the capacity to adapt to the business, and its overall environment, while bringing new skills to a project, team, or organization. They are very different from the type of employees you hire to maintain a mature business.

If you are in a turnaround situation in which your company needs a new direction or is in distress, hiring is about finding the right people with the technical skills and knowledge to set your company back on the right course.

Hiring and Job Search in the New World of Work

Today, it is easier than ever for candidates to identify new job opportunities. Therefore, as a leader, you need to concentrate on hiring new talent while keeping your current employees engaged—some of whom may spend their lunch breaks looking for new jobs on their smartphones. Not only is it easier than ever to look for a job, but also the trend toward a "gig economy" is accelerating. The gig economy, or freelancing, refers to temporary workers taking on roles for specific projects with predetermined timelines and rates. The term "gig" originated in the music industry but has now taken on a wider meaning, as people are breaking away from steady employment in search of what they see as freedom and flexibility. Freelancers in the gig economy may be working in an industry where they have established themselves, more akin to consultants, or in new ventures with companies like Uber or TaskRabbit.

MIND SWITCH FACT

According to a 2015 Jobvite survey (*Job Seeker Nation Study*, February), job seeking is now a 24/7 activity: job seekers search for new positions on mobile devices during their commute (38 percent), on the job (30 percent), and even in the bathroom (18 percent).

> **"Knowing how to hire, understanding the traits that matter most to you, and realizing how good and bad hiring impacts your success are all crucial to being a good leader."**

With technology, freelancing has become easier and more viable than in previous generations. This concept of freedom from permanent commitment, while still making a living, can be hard to compete with when you're looking for full-time employees in a traditional office environment. Related, the era of one company and one job, for an extended period of time, is long gone for many people in the workplace. Talent is mobile and in high demand, and the contemporary workforce may act more like free agents than corporate citizens.

MIND SWITCH FACT

In a survey commissioned by Upwork and the Freelancers Union, "Freelancing in America: 2016," it is estimated that there are 55 million people in the United States working freelance in some capacity. This is up 1 million people from a similar study in 2015—also commissioned by the Freelancers Union.

As a leader you will need to embrace these trends, understanding not only how to work with members of the gig economy, but also to attract steady talent to your cause or company. Leaders need to differentiate themselves and their businesses from others, highlighting their strengths throughout the hiring process. Keep in mind, even though leaders must be tough and thorough in their hiring process, it is more of a two-way dating game than ever before. Good hiring managers know they are "on show" just as much as the candidate.

In our experience, talented candidates like a hiring process that feels as if they will have to stretch themselves to get the offer, but they also like to feel that they are getting "sold to"—as compared to simply getting quizzed or tested on their background, knowledge, and skills. Today's best candidates wait for no one since they have more options than ever before. As a hiring manger, you must therefore be ready to make decisions on potential hires efficiently. Even if you need some time to decide, however, providing quick updates on the hiring process will go a long way to establishing good candidate rapport. This simple act of proactive communication on the progress of an interview process cannot be stressed enough; it is good etiquette and also a signal that you are serious about your talent strategy. Sadly, in our experience this proactive communication happens less often than we would like.

MIND SWITCH FACT

According to Investopedia Online Trading Academy (July 1, 2016), the top ways to find a job are:
Networking
Referrals
Job boards and career websites
Job fairs
Company websites
Cold calling
Headhunters and recruitment agencies
Temping and internships
Creative or outlandish tactics

Hiring Biases to Avoid

In today's multigenerational business landscape, managers are hiring from a wide-ranging candidate list comprised of people with many different skills and backgrounds. No matter what generational category you fall under, you must be able to make the best decision possible: it's necessary to ignore stereotypes, assess exactly what you need in the role you're filling, and have a plan for onboarding once you make the decision. Though there is a tendency for our brains to make quick judgments, and let bias creep into the interview process, good leaders will be enlightened and dynamic when it comes to identifying and hiring talent. They will come to the decision with open minds, leaving behind preconceived notions, stereotypical responses, or biases based on their previous experiences, such as hiring someone similar to them; not hiring someone who could be a threat to their status in the organization; superficial stereotyping because of tattoos, body weight, or age; or confirming what they already believe to be either positive or negative about the person.

To assist them along the way, hiring managers should carefully include others in the process to help mitigate against their own biases and build a team that brings unique assets to the table (instead of hiring their own personal "mini-mes"). But they shouldn't be tempted to have too many others involved! Bringing perspective from outside the specific domain being interviewed for will also be beneficial. Ideally, the people they include are widely read and informed, see context as important to any situation, and draw on more than their own experiences to make decisions.

After consulting others, if you find that a candidate has the capabilities for the role, the experience required, and the right temperament, ask yourself: (1) Can I imagine communicating the reasons for this person's promotion in 12 months' time, and what would I be saying? This will help you clarify in your mind the candidate's strongest attributes and how they are complementary to the team. And (2) what does the candidate's résumé gain from this role? This question will help you find win-win hires. If you can answer these two questions with clarity, you probably should hire the person. It is your role to make thoughtful

"When I look at you I ask myself, 'How would this person reflect on me?' If I recommend you and back you, I want you to make me look good in my decision making."

decisions, but not to dither, so know that at some point, the diligence has to stop and it's time to make a decision.

When making an offer, you need to clearly show candidates how they can immediately contribute to the team and company while also taking advantage of development opportunities for their own careers and personal goals. This part of the hiring process isn't about the compensation (that's the hook), it's about attracting candidates to dig further and ask more questions (it's the bait). This will make for a more positive on-boarding experience, if they accept the position, and a clearer understanding of what you are both entering into.

Being Prepared

In addition to fully understanding and executing on the hiring process, leaders should maintain a team that includes a "pipeline" of potential candidates for different roles that they can get to know over time. As a manager, you are not just hiring for today, you are also hiring for tomorrow, and a rapidly changing environment necessitates your proactivity. Creating this pipeline will also help you refine your views on the characteristics and skills needed for each role and potentially lead to a fast hiring process if timing and circumstances line up accordingly.

Another way to stay prepared is to articulate to candidates what it would take to succeed in the role *before* you interview them. Note that this explanation is different from the job spec, which is more about skills and experiences to get the candidates in the door. Not only will this help the potential hires understand the role, but it also will help you think about how the best candidates might be able raise the performance of your team and company overall.

Lastly, leaders need to invest in managing the process aspect of hiring early and then stick to it. Discipline is needed in this process to avoid a feast and famine cycle of having to desperately ignite a candidate pipeline when you are starving for talent or getting lazy when you are in the good times of having a fully staffed team.

As we mentioned, involving others, communicating actively, and deciding swiftly can all work in your favor, but good process will make sure hiring is seamless and repeatable. And remember, it's up to you as the hiring manager or leader: you can't blame your HR partner if you miss a desirable candidate through sloppy execution. The people with their necks on the line have to take responsibility, and if you're the leader, then that's you, and you'd better be ready. Your next hire could raise the performance and output of the whole team—or contribute to its demise. If it's the latter, you may find yourself in the unfortunate position of having to remove someone from the team or company, or if you're not living up to your duties and expectations as a hiring manager, then you, too, could end up being unceremoniously deposited back into the candidate pool elsewhere.

Firing Employees

From our own experiences managing and coaching hundreds of sophisticated executives throughout different industries and geographies, we've learned that the days when managers and leaders need to let people go are the darkest and most challenging ones. And, unfortunately, the act of firing someone rarely gets easier with time. It doesn't matter whether it is because of economic circumstances, ongoing performance issues, lack of adherence to values, or because someone made a serious mistake—firing employees is tough.

It is important to remember, however, that making the decision to let someone go is, at times, essential to a team's existence and success. If you have good ethics and strong performance management philosophies, and if you care deeply about having the right people in the right roles and doing the right thing by the whole team, you will make the right decision. You need to think about the long-term health and growth of your team or company and use all information available to help your people reach their full potential. The firing process is about unblocking the team dynamics, removing underperformers or those with jaded attitudes to allow a better outcome for the broader enterprise.

Handling Today's Challenges

As with many issues discussed throughout this book, technology advances and demographic changes demand that leaders make decisions faster and more accurately. Though advice about making tough choices, such as who to let go and when, is generally timeless, these two factors affect a team's talent in a whole new way.

For example, repetitive tasks currently performed by humans are becoming automated. Instead of endless, slow-moving meetings, big data is being used to make decisions. Software is becoming increasingly intelligent, making certain roles redundant. In this era, underperformers are more obvious than ever before as serious attention is given to the specific roles humans play in any product or service development. The human touch is still needed in regard to creativity and collaboration—and developing these among your top performers is critical to success—but many positions are becoming obsolete. This new reality heightens the need for good judgment on retaining the best employees and letting go those that aren't cutting it. For employees, it means you need to be more enlightened than ever and be ready to adapt to the environment and reskill if you are in a position that is likely to be disrupted by automation or artificial intelligence.

MIND SWITCH FACT

In 2015 the Committee for Economic Development of Australia (CEDA) released a report on the future of work in Australia in which it concluded that computerization and automation would replace 40 percent of roles in the Australian workforce in the next 15 years. That is as many as 5 million jobs. Surveys in Asia, Europe, the United States, and the United Kingdom predict a similar narrative.

In the United States, Forrester's tech researchers estimated that technological innovation will mean the end to 9.1 million jobs by 2025. When the World Economic Forum (WEF) met in the Swiss Alps in 2015, it surveyed

15 countries—accounting for 65 percent of the world's workforce—and found that 7.1 million jobs would be lost to robotics in the next five years (*The Future of Work*). Irrespective of the study you read, the direction is the same and the pace is fast.

Even if you aren't in an industry where artificial intelligence or robots are likely to replace large swaths of employees anytime soon, the pressure to have the best possible team at all times is at historic highs. Moreover, the likelihood that you will have to let someone go for errors that may have been overlooked in the past is also high due to today's socially connected world and the channels that we now operate in as employees and in our personal lives. The new world of work is simply more complicated than it used to be. Consider for a minute that 24 hours a day, the people you work with have the potential to make mistakes or act in ways that could damage your company. Previously, many of these actions went unnoticed or under the radar, but with the Internet and its endless social media platforms, anything an employee does, inside or outside the office, is likely to be documented in one way or another (remember, the same goes for you!).

As a leader this can be scary, but the only solution is to have great systems and values in place for your team, ones that they fully understand and agree upon. Inevitably, however, some employees slip up. Therefore, you must be ready to stay strong when you are needed to act on talent decisions, and to let people go when the decision has been made. The best leaders we have interacted with during our careers have all demonstrated their generosity to help those people that they must let go. They suggest actions like doubling a company's severance policy, and they encourage companies to help people find their new paths after they leave.

Of course, the actual firing is never pleasant, and there are many employees you will never hear from again after they leave. You can't control what happens after they're gone, but you can control how you conduct yourself at the time. You must make the moment as dignified as possible. For example, think ahead about whether they need to leave the building immediately, and if so, offer to meet them in the parking lot with their purse or bag and ask if there are special items they would like shipped overnight. Also, choose the location carefully to ensure that the risk of anyone walking in or seeing the meeting is minimized. It is also imperative to never breathe a word to anyone else about the reasons, timing, or circumstances of an employee's removal. The most important reason for this is that it's not truly anyone else's business except for those people directly involved in the decision-making process. Secondarily as a leader, anything you say can be misinterpreted by other staff or employees. The cues you give need to be about the future and about the remaining team members, so their confidence in their own positions and abilities stays intact and they keep focus.

> "If you are slow or indecisive in firing, you will be faced with a nasty scenario of losing your top performers because you kept your weakest. It doesn't help anyone to do this."

The new world of work is demanding, and as we have discussed, there are complications we deal with now, including tech advances, that mean some jobs are simply going away and others will require different skills. It may also mean that the frequency of leaders letting people go may increase.

When you are faced with the situation of having to tell someone that their role is no longer open to them, you may feel guilty or bad about the circumstances and be tempted to talk too much, try to explain the context in detail, or be apologetic for the incident at hand. These are natural feelings, but trying to be overly nice will only make things worse. "Nice" is like beauty, it's in the eye of the beholder. Due to the nature of the likely emotional situation, your intent and impact of trying to be nice won't be in sync. Aim for high integrity and respectfulness.

Being "nice" could also open an aperture where the person being fired may try to convince you to take a different path, you may then say something that increases liability for your organization, or you will create further distress by hinting that you don't own the decision. When it comes to moving people out of your enterprise, remember that it is not about *you*, so don't try to be "nice" about it, just be respectful. Remain pleasantly assertive and clearly and concisely deliver the news. Then introduce the right person at the company to talk about available resources to help the person move forward—this is the only method we have seen to be effective.

In regard to demographic changes, shifts in balance across different generations (including the rise of the millennials) have led to increasing demands for stretch opportunities from rising stars on any team. In the meantime, many workers are not adapting as well to the technologically advanced, globalized world. Not everyone is as dedicated to his or her own development as former U.S. Secretary of Defense Donald Rumsfeld, who according to *Time* magazine, at 83 has just developed his first videogame app called Churchill Solitaire. He said, "Whatever one's age, the courage to leave one's comfort zone is the most crucial factor of all." (January 2016, *Donald Rumsfeld, You're No Winston Churchill*)

The demographic shifts we are seeing mean leaders need to decide what they value the most on their teams, and what kind of generational makeup will contribute to the highest levels of success. Ideally, there will be appreciation for both deep experience *and* fresh, innovative ideas, but there are times when you may need to make difficult decisions on what's best for your company. When budgets are tightened or revenues are low and investors or superiors are poking around asking about the inflated salaries of longtime employees on one hand, or inexperienced, green employees on the other, it is likely that you'll be called upon to justify everyone on your team. It's not easy, but there are ways to make the process of constant rebalancing of skills and experience more effective and to be proactive about the composition of your team ahead of being asked. Firing underperformers is just one element of this proactivity; managers also need to keep motivation high at all times.

MIND SWITCH FACT

According to a 2013 Gallup study of more than 140 countries, only one in eight employees was "psychologically committed to their jobs and likely to be making positive contributions to their organizations." This leaves 63 percent of employees studied in the "not engaged" category (*State of the Global Workplace*). In a similar Gallup study of the U.S. workforce that surveyed more than 80,000 people, Gallup found that 35 percent of employees were engaged. They also found that 50.8 percent are not engaged.

The rising stars on your team will be particularly adept at sensing your leadership strength around talent and how dynamic you are willing to be to create opportunities for the rest of the team. If they observe peers or superiors "mailing it in" or simply unengaged, you will lose their respect and, with it, the opportunity to lead them. They may do what you say, but they won't follow you in the same way as if they respected and trusted your judgment.

> **"Remain strong when times are tough, and be willing to take leaps even when failure is an option."**

Even with all the greatest advice on firing in the world, it is still emotionally a very hard thing to do. Many people feel a sense of loyalty to individual team members or respect the loyalty that they have had toward the company. Unfortunately, loyalty isn't always enough. Garnering respect and trust from your bosses and other employees hinges on your willingness to keep your bar high and make these tough calls. Once you're able to do so, other leadership tasks will come easier.

Time Off

The concept of time off—vacation, personal days, and sick days—may seem antiquated for entrepreneurial companies that live in an "always on" world where their employees' tablets or smartphones are akin to extra appendages. Even for more traditional companies, where time off is a necessary employment benefit, dividing work and personal time with a clear line can still be hard, leading to potentially uncomfortable discussions between bosses and employees.

In the new world of work, telecommuting and remote work is becoming the norm and connectivity is 24/7. In some ways, "time off" almost feels false in this era. Still, there are diverse views on how much employee's personal lives should bleed into work and vice versa. Demands and expectations of different generations and cultures vary greatly, and as a leader, the respect for diversity of needs and wants relating to personal time away from work is crucial. This makes managing expectations around hours worked and protecting leisure time for both yourself and your team increasingly difficult. We believe it is also an area most in need of a mind switch.

Supporting Balance

One of our former colleagues refers to a "work-life blender" when talking about the blurred lines between business and pleasure and the expectation that employees, and managers, are always available. The "work-life blender" brings a smile to our faces as we conjure up the image of some concoction of fruits and vegetables meant to be good for you. This "concoction" is what great leaders should seek: a solution that is healthy and infused with different ingredients for success—both time to work hard and time to recharge.

Today's leaders need to be enlightened and know that with the rise of Gen Y and Gen Z employees it is wise to treat them like individuals and manage them as such. If you are resisting the changes, make the mind switch now. The change is here, and embracing it is the only real option. Being playful around how you integrate work and life and leading by example, instead of blindly leaning on rules and regulations, can be extraordinarily powerful. Related, valuing an environment of empowerment and results over and above prescriptive requests about how and when your teams work will produce greater results. There is no one perfect way to manage the needs of employees and company goals, but enlightened and playful leaders build a culture that enables different generations and styles in the workforce. They understand that different employees will have different levels of comfort around asking for time off and every person's demands outside of work are different and complicated in their own way.

Open communication about time-off expectations and company standards will allow everyone to better plan their personal and work schedules, leading to less potential confusion, misunderstanding, or resentment. In the process, as a leader, you must engage your employees and support them. One of the best things you can say to your top team members is "I haven't noticed any time-off requests from you in a while. Do you have any upcoming plans? I know you've been working hard." This simple statement will alleviate your employees' concerns that their work ethic is not noticed or appreciated or that any upcoming vacation might be denied. This small gesture can be powerful irrespective of whether you think "time off" is for the manufacturing line or from another era.

If your company has time-off policies, don't assume that your team isn't working when they are on vacation or away from the office. Ignoring those employees who go above and beyond is folly, and every employee needs downtime. Good leaders give their teams clear permission and support to recharge and enjoy themselves. They also suggest backup plans for their responsibilities while they are out to make sure they feel at ease. When they return, leaders who are kindly confident politely ask about their trip, or even to see a selfie if appropriate, and take a genuine interest.

MIND SWITCH FACT

A survey of employed e-mail users finds:

22 percent are expected to respond to work e-mail when they're not at work.

50 percent check work e-mail on the weekends.

46 percent check work e-mail on sick days.

34 percent check work e-mail while on vacation.

(September 2013, American Psychological Association, *Americans Stay Connected to Work on Weekend, Vacations, and Even When Out Sick*)

Spectrum of Time-Off Norms

Time-off norms vary widely across geographies, companies, and industries. Having lived and worked on three different continents and in 18 countries, we can vouch for the wide spectrum of views on this topic. We all know that working too much is bad for us, but in some industries, geographies, and demographics it is applauded as professionally heroic and a sign of commitment to the company (and sometimes to capitalism itself).

Moving to New York City from London (and being Australian) was a particular shock for Kylie in terms of how U.S. companies viewed time off. In London, and throughout Europe, most employees are legally allowed more than five weeks paid time off, not including national holidays. In her home country of Australia, four weeks is the legal amount of paid vacation time. Kylie was therefore surprised to find New Yorkers taking vacation apologetically with certain unwritten rules around how time off could be applied. This is partly because of law, where the United States is the only OECD country where there is no legal requirement to provide for paid vacation time, but also because of culture. In

New York, the most acceptable norm among Kylie's peers was to take a week over the summer. Taking two weeks in succession was virtually unheard of unless the person was getting married. Further, people regularly bragged about how much stored up time off they had according to the HR system, which is akin to bragging about how little sleep you have had or how many hot dogs you can eat in one sitting.

This extreme version of "aversion to time off" is changing quickly in some industries and geographies. In fact, there is currently hot debate around whether specified time off is necessary at all anymore, or whether it is an administrative hurdle no longer needed. The trend toward management teams removing structured time-off policies—essentially granting unlimited vacation days—is one that is taking hold and expected to continue.

While companies like Netflix are leading the charge with unlimited vacation day policies, the idea has been around for quite some time. The first instance of unlimited vacation that we have researched dates back to 1981. In this example, the Brazilian company Semco is reported to have adopted unlimited vacation when the son of the founder suffered from health issues and realized that his work habits were contributing to them. He decided to remove scheduled sick days and vacation time and was rewarded by his employees with greater results and loyalty. More recently, other companies such as LinkedIn and General Electric have followed Netflix's lead, implementing similar unlimited vacation policies in 2015.

Keeping Employees Happy

Companies are constantly challenged to step up their competitiveness to attract and retain talent. One way to do so is by updating time-off policies and providing your employees with new options to help them balance, integrate, or at least juggle their work and personal lives. At the heart of the idea, you're simply trying to keep your employees happy and productive. If giving them a few extra days, or even weeks, off, or letting them design their own schedules results in better performance, you'd be amiss as a leader to not take advantage of changing time-off expectations.

Make sure you stay current, researching and following trends within leading-edge companies to start conversations with your peers and other leaders around this topic. Ask your management teams if they believe a fresh approach to time off can attract and motivate the best talent, while also showing good governance and oversight. It is, of course, a fine balance and takes great communication of expectations and confidence in your teams to successfully navigate changes in your policies and potentially in your culture. As with all trends, unlimited vacation, for example, may not be right for your company—there are instances in which companies have implemented unlimited vacation policies and then reversed the decision—but keeping astride with changing attitudes and company policies will help you better develop the right policies for your own organization.

Lastly, be cognizant of how management of employees' time can impact morale and ultimately productivity. Employees know that the 24/7 demands of today's workforce are new and different and are likely trying to wrestle down their own opinion on how they can succeed in such an environment. Be supportive and help them along the way, making sure that, no matter how your time-off policies are structured, your employees are comfortable with the situation and receiving the time and resources they need to produce the best results at work. And remember, they have plenty of other things to worry about while in the office—like a list of seemingly endless meetings.

Hosting Meetings

Even the best leaders don't like meetings any more than anyone else, but they are simply a sticky fact of office life. Perhaps one day our virtual collaboration tools and other workplace effectiveness solutions will evolve to the point where meetings become extinct, but until then, the best way to approach required meetings is to make them brief and effective by first explaining to everyone who must attend, why the meeting is necessary, and "what's in it for them." Then together, leaders and their teams must debate, discuss, think, and come out with recommendations on how to move forward. Leaders must maintain their kindly confidence during meetings and use everyone's time productively. This skill is a major one and can save, or suck, time from your life and the lives of your team.

MIND SWITCH FACT

The *Atlantic* reports on a 2014 survey from AtTask (conducted by Harris Poll) that found that U.S. employees at large companies (1,000 employees or more) only spend 45 percent of their time on primary job duties—40 percent of their working hours were spent on meetings, administrative tasks, and "interruptions." This is a huge commitment, most likely justified in the spirit of "collaboration" or "information sharing" or "consensus building."

In-Person Meetings

In-person meetings (as opposed to virtual meetings or one-to-one conversations) still have a place in today's busy world, but in our view they should be the outlier in any one given working week. As an uber-communicative leader, you already know that you should be using all channels to connect with your team, peers, and customers, sharing knowledge and making decisions, therefore in-person meetings are less necessary than ever before. Some leaders unfortunately claim that meetings contribute toward completing a goal, when in reality many just waste time. Good leaders don't lie to themselves, or their team, about the effectiveness of frivolous meetings—as Ernest Hemingway used to say, "Never mistake motion for action."

When good leaders do call an in-person meeting, they are mindful of the intention and laser focused on getting to the necessary results. They are playful when appropriate, and confident in their delivery. They call meetings only at times when everyone needs to look each other in the eye to be able to make decisions or because there is an emphasized need for team bonding over an issue or opportunity that has arisen. Even in the fourth revolution the human touch will be more important than ever, but meetings are not the only way to express your humanity—they may even produce the opposite result! This negative outcome of meetings occurs when people use meetings as their platform to whine or complain, when devices are used to stave off boredom instead of focusing on the task at hand, or when leaders get frustrated with group dynamics in a meeting and unleash their temper in a public setting.

No executive has ever proclaimed, "We need more meetings"—meetings turn either productive or unproductive based on the prethinking or planning and the discipline in execution.

Getting the Most out of Meetings

Dynamic leaders display energy when they walk into a room to host a meeting. They have an agenda prepared and acknowledge the views of everyone in attendance. They seek perspectives from all corners and encourage everyone to participate. In fact, in our experience, some of the quietest people in the room might end up being the most insightful. Effective meeting managers also start meetings on time and insist on everyone being present, both physically and mentally—sometimes you have to tell your team members to leave their devices at their desks. These managers lead by example and know that everyone's time is precious. That said, being present doesn't have to mean being in the room. In the globally distributed new world of work, using Skype or Google Hangouts or your approved conference system is an equally effective way to reach everyone that is needed.

An effective leader will be the first in the meeting, working when others arrive, will ask questions versus giving direction, and will be the first to leave, stating to instill confidence: "You guys have got it. It's in your hands." An example of a great leader that we have observed asks everyone present at the start of a regular meeting that he holds with his team, "Is there any reason that anyone here today can't contribute fully to this time together?" This allows people who have a major issue going on that might distract them to talk openly about their current mindset and also signals that his expectations are high for everyone's full attention.

One successful approach to meetings that we particularly like comes from Jack Dorsey, CEO of Twitter & Square. In a 2016 interview with *Fortune* (March, *How Twitter CEO Jack Dorsey Plans to Fix the Company*), Dorsey discussed how he compresses meetings on particular themes in one day. For example, Mondays are for operational issues, Tuesdays for product development, and Thursdays to boost productivity. We don't recommend necessarily having these meetings every week, but the concept of creating themes around meetings, and keeping them consistent, will help your employees be prepared and organized and will make the meetings quicker and less painful. The predictability also allows for the rhythm of the organization to potentially keep pace with its leader.

MIND SWITCH FACT

According to a study published by University of Missouri researchers in the *Journal of Applied Psychology*, "standing-up meetings," in which participants stand during the discussion, can reduce the time taken to conduct a meeting by up to 66 percent.

Whether in a group or individual meeting, leaders must specify the purpose and stated goal of that meeting. Keep in mind that there is a lot of noise to compete with—deadlines, e-mails, new clients, phone calls, complaints from customers, and so on—so don't let the point of the meeting, or the meeting itself, be drowned out. Specify what the meetings are about, for example revenues, marketing, or operations, as compared to "check-in" meetings across an entire team. Then set context for a meeting with supporting materials in

> "The only people who like meetings are the people who call them. Everyone thinks their meetings are special, but they're not. Recognize that nobody wants to be there. Be productive and concise."

the days before, allowing everyone to enter the room informed and prepared to maximize their time together. In our view, since information exchange can happen virtually now, leaders should only use meetings to make decisions and to contribute to productivity.

Whatever principle you use to organize the meetings you host, you must stick to the three guiding principles of meetings: timeliness, agendas, and follow-up. Meetings should produce clear results, contributing to the actual performance of the team, avoid wasting time, and lead to the best decisions possible.

The Mind Switch on Basic Leadership Responsibilities

While we have called this chapter the basics of leadership, these aren't necessarily easy topics. They are essential to master but also fraught with so many potential mistakes. In hiring and firing, making mistakes can lead to financial damage and reputation risk, while poorly managing time-off culture or hosting wasteful meetings can be motivation killers. For these reasons, all leaders should devote time and energy to thinking about how effectively they are managing these aspects of their role and consider how they need to change in the new world of work. In particular, they should ask themselves if they are abreast of the most current thinking around policies and trends that are producing superior productivity. Acquiring and keeping the best talent relies on leaders embracing change and flowing with it. These are not areas of management to be swimming upstream. Even if your organization is not exhibiting urgency in the methods it uses in basic leadership to keep up with tech and demographic changes, you as a leader should do so. The most important leadership behaviors needed to make a mind switch on these topics are being uber-communicative and kindly confident.

STORIES FROM THE ROAD

Two Gen Zs in business school weigh in on their leadership expectations.

ALYSSA KHAN

I think that with the fast-changing technology the work-life balance is being decreased in a way. I believe this because since everyone has their smartphone basically attached to their bodies at all times, I think that personal life is bleeding into work life. I believe this because with the developing technology, the usage with different social media applications is being increased. As we know, a main reason for social media is for personal benefit and connections. I also believe that with the technology and the usage of these social media applications increasing, the boundaries between coworkers and even employees and higher-up leaders is being decreased. Often you see that with Facebook, Twitter, and Instagram (along with all of the other applications), employees are "friending" other employees and their higher-ups. Since their social media pages are not just professional (usually) these boundaries between work life and home life are being decreased because all of the information on the page can be seen by basically anyone.

As far as the leadership quality of being a good communicator goes, I believe that with the increasing development of technology, communication in general is both increasing and decreasing. I think that it is increasing because now there are so many ways to reach a person, whenever you want. For example, phone calls, text messages, e-mails, social media platforms. So in this instance I think that the technology development is a good thing. On the other side, I think that the use of technology is making us (in general) poor communicators. With the use of written messages like texts and e-mails, people are getting the idea that they can be short and/or informal and maybe not take a conversation as seriously as if it were face-to-face or a phone call.

SORCHA MOLDAUER

I would have to agree with the mixed ages and cultures dramatically influencing the leadership requirements now and in years to come. As well as the technology, alas, I haven't any idea where technology will take us (even next year).

I agree with all of your proposed traits, and would like to add to a couple of them.

First, communication. I believe that a "good communicator" is someone who is able to provide *relevant* and *timely* feedback. Meaning, rather than waiting for an annual review, or a monthly review, the leader is constantly noticing followers' behavior, and correcting immediately, or praising immediately. There is a book that claims millennials want feedback—but only positive feedback, and I disagree. From my personal experience, feedback is only helpful if constructive, which means that negative feedback must be given. At my last job, I was a lead teller at a bank. A position that was halfway between teller and manager. I had taken PTO and ended up getting dreadfully ill on my trip

(I was hospitalized for a number of days). However, my first day back I went into work, not realizing exactly how sick I was. I told one of our regulars that I wasn't feeling particularly well, and that I thought I had gotten some kind of flu. According to my manager, other customers overheard my comment, and gave my manager a disapproving glance. I went into work the next day, and my manager said nothing of it. I was hospitalized, and called out for three days, and on the fourth day I went back to work and was pulled aside and given a write-up. She claimed that me telling my regular that I was ill was unprofessional, and completely inappropriate. I was confused, and felt as though she had failed me as a leader for not helping me recognize and correct my behavior immediately.

Confidence and courage to make decisions go hand in hand. However, I also think that for our generation, it's important to keep us informed. If there isn't a reason to be keeping things on the down-low, I know millennials appreciate being informed, and not being blindsided by a leader's decision.

In addition to being intellectually curious and always learning, also influencing and encouraging this in their followers.

Yes! We want to be empowered. Give us a task and let us fly. We have spent so many years in school following strict rubrics and being unable to express ourselves creatively. Give us that opportunity, and most of us will not disappoint!

Work-life balance is difficult. I believe that many leaders have to understand that our generation grew up with everything changing constantly; thus we expect that in our careers. I think it's more of a flaw on our part, rather than a leader who may be from a different time.

Charisma is difficult for me, because I want my leaders to be *authentic*. Many times, I have found that a charismatic leader comes off as plastic or fake, not truly showing who they are.

Just the personality that they believe will inspire people to get things done. Maybe we need to create a new word that means both charismatic and authentic. (An example: in our recent presidential race, we had several candidates on the Republican side who come across as very *charismatic*, however, they don't seem *authentic or trustworthy* to me.)

〈〈〈〉〉〉

Cheryl Flink, chief strategy officer, Market Force, writes about letting go of assumptions.

Market Force manages a base of several hundred thousand independent contractors around the globe who conduct audits and mystery shops. They are the eyes and ears for large multilocation brands that want to assess compliance with brand standards across thousands of sites. In the past five years, the demographics of this group—and the way they interact with technology—have shifted dramatically. This shift includes millennials who require high touch communication through social media—and they've moved well beyond Twitter and Facebook. In addition, nearly the entire base uses smartphones. We are constantly challenged to remain relevant and have responded to changing needs for technology with mobile apps and new communication touch points.

A key challenge for our leadership team? Letting go of assumptions. Take privacy as an example. News articles lament the lack of privacy in today's "always on" society where technology can track our every move. However, most smartphone users—especially millennials—accept that they give up privacy in order to have access to functions that make their lives more interesting, fun, or efficient. The opportunity to share experiences is highly prized. These key points are true today—but could literally change overnight as new opinions, attitudes, and technology come to life.

To cope with the speed of change, leaders must develop a "fast pipe" of information to track technology changes, adoption rates, and perceived benefits for both their internal teams and external customers. That fast pipe can be used to shape the nuanced marketing communications required for a global team. It can shape the responses of a nimble technology team tasked with quick development life cycles. And it can become the funnel of ideas that informs strategy. The last thing leaders want is to be caught flat-footed.

There's perhaps no better example of missing the changes in demographics than the quick serve restaurant (QSR) industry. Many QSRs have focused on value—putting a premium on a very affordable price rather than really great food. Enter fast casual restaurants that reverse that equation: really great food for a pretty good—but not cheap—price. Millennials embraced that new value equation and turned the QSR industry upside down. They want good food, and they don't mind paying for it. And there's more to come.

Because millennials embrace technology, they're very comfortable with ordering and paying for their food with a smartphone app or tabletop technology. That could have a very disruptive impact on the restaurant industry. The days of needing waitstaff to take an order and bring the bill may become a fond memory. To remain competitive, restaurant leaders must face that reality—and that may mean painful decisions about the size and relevance of their service workforce.

07

CREATING CULTURE IN THE NEW WORLD OF WORK

Though the basic leadership tasks discussed in Chapter 6 are fairly concrete, as a manager and leader, you'll be expected to perform less tangible ones as well. The value of a company depends on the quality of its leadership: it is that simple. And arguably, one of the most important roles the leadership team plays within a company or enterprise is to foster a productive, positive culture, one that enhances the brand, improves the ability to recruit employees into the company and retain them, and delivers results reliably.

MIND SWITCH FACT

A 2015 *Fortune* magazine headline read, "The best employers in the U.S. say their greatest tool is culture." The story went on to report that "leaders of the 100 Best Companies 2015 to work for know the secret to business success is not just about earnings, but about creating an ideal culture for their employees."

Yet the definition of "culture" is tricky. Many say it is the character and personality of a company. Others argue that "culture" comes from the top, ideas or behaviors passed down from founders or high-level executives, and some define it as "what happens when no one is watching." In our experience, workplace culture is the "aura" of a team within a company, those subtle, ubiquitous qualities or the general atmosphere that informs people on how to act. A company's culture seeps from the walls, and it isn't dependent on any one person or workplace perk. It slowly builds but can be quickly harmed. Culture is a mystical yet real feature of any organization. Using this lens, culture cannot be gamed or directed—it simply is what it is, but it can be influenced and evolved over time.

The Complexity of Company Culture

In our experience, Peter Drucker's famous quote "Culture eats strategy for breakfast" has definitely played out to be true. We have seen product failures that were strategically destined to succeed but couldn't get off the ground because

their launch was not suitably planned with the cultural elements of the company in mind. We have also seen great talent
rejected from an organization—at steep financial and psychological cost—because they couldn't survive in that
particular culture.

A common example of such rejection happens when
maturing companies try to reach the next level of scale by
hiring rock star, "big company" talent. Many times, the new
'big company' talent understand the
dynamics of change and how to manage
bigger budgets, teams, and problems,
but they can't develop the social capital needed to succeed in a team that
has probably built something from
scratch together and has a culture of
loyalty first. Another example is when
great technical product experts are on-
boarded into a team that values sales
acumen above all else. This situation

> "As a leader you must understand your company's culture and set the tone such that the culture is a positive force and hopefully a competitive advantage."

can lead to difficult interactions about how to develop the
product to a higher level and can ultimately result in a failure
to integrate someone who was carefully hired. Product and
sales playing nicely together is imperative for success, and if
a power struggle occurs, the results can be disastrous.

Seemingly fundamentally sound companies have even
spiraled into decline because of flaws in their cultures—you
need look no further than the Lehman Brothers of the finance
industry or the VWs of the automobile industry to find some
prime examples. As we write this book, the Wells Fargo culture is in the public eye for a sales culture that ignored ethics
to reach its goals and has been accused of opening new
accounts for clients without their permission (and worse!).

> **"The culture must be easily observed and consistent. It can't be bought or faked."**

When sketchy ethics are embedded as part of the cultural makeup of a company, or risky shortcuts are deemed acceptable, long-run failure is inevitable in our opinion. Of course, no company culture wants to include "failure" as a main tenant, so people end up lying to cover up their mistakes, only leading to further potentially disastrous results.

On the flip side, there are many seemingly good companies where the culture is questionable but the commercial success is unhindered. For example, Goldman Sachs, Amazon, and Walmart have all been occasionally looked at with skepticism due to the companies' demands on its employees and vendors. But they are large and financially successful companies that produce important products and services. This shows the multifaceted nature of companies and how culture is not the only determinant of success. These companies are often well regarded by their customers and have arguably stayed above board in their practices thus far.

Reconciling these observations confirms the complexity of company culture—in fact, it's nearly impossible to make black-and-white statements in this area. The only certainty is that as a leader you must have a dedicated, solid view on the culture you want to foster, the current state of that culture within your company, and what you need to further instill and develop that culture in the future.

Directing Culture

As a leader, you can direct your company's culture in different ways: whether you want to make it fun, serious, intense, laid-back, meritocratic, or cutthroat, you have the ability to push the company in a certain direction. But you shouldn't mistake your role as the person to specifically define the culture—you may be able to help foster it, but as only one person you'll never have the final say on how it plays out. And unless you are the CEO, there are many other leaders subtly influencing the culture day to day as well.

The size of a company and its stage of development can be factors in how easy or difficult it is to direct a culture. The smaller the company, the more powerful individual personalities can be on any one team and the more likely it is for bad actors to damage a culture, or for good people to enhance it. In larger companies, it's more difficult for individuals to single-handedly influence the culture. This element of large company management puts a higher onus on management teams to set the example to live by and intentionally set the tone they want the company to follow.

Directing and shaping company culture is an important part of the fourth revolution leader's suite of capabilities. Keep in mind, though, that your vision of the culture and the reality need to connect. For example, if you want to attract millennials with a less traditional, more playful culture, you need to make sure your colleagues are on board. If you have a foosball table that no one ever plays because employees know that one of the tyrannical executive team members would frown on any such frivolity, you have lost already. If you want to foster playfulness, you must be willing to try new things. Any misalignment between the image and the reality will be quickly found out. The more you simply talk about culture, the less your version of it may be true. You must lead by example.

You also need to constantly assess your company's culture and whether or not it is on the right track to success. Asking new employees to describe the culture as they see it during on-boarding is perhaps the most likely path to a realistic assessment on how your culture is being shaped at any point in time. Checking in with other employees can also prove fruitful. You must be personally engaged in the surrounding culture, or you'll never really know what's going on, nor how to direct it one way or another if necessary. In any company culture, though, there are a number of traits that will confidently lead to the most productive teams and organization overall.

A Culture of Inclusion and Diversity

In our view, inclusion and diversity are about developing the best ideas and finding the right people to deliver on them. Such a culture doesn't exclude anyone based on background or circumstances, and it remains flexible to find positive ways to get the best out of people. An inclusive, diverse culture contributes to the broadest range of views and different ways of doing things, which undoubtedly leads to interesting, innovative ideas and processes.

You cannot deny the positive benefits to having more diverse thought in your talent pool in the demanding new world of work, nor can you deny the importance of your workplace reflecting your customer base—every industry's customers are becoming increasingly diverse. Admittedly, having many different views can cause the decision-making process to sometimes be slower, and maybe messier, due to greater debate and a longer time spent understanding

"Get better yourself, but make your team and project better too."

fresh and unique thoughts and considerations. But in the long run, the outcomes will be stronger and better.

Very simply, diversity of thought, and an inclusive culture that fosters such thought, mitigates against groupthink and brings ideas from the edge to the center of conversations because such a culture will be open to, instead of skeptical of, radically different thinking. Being an inclusive leader means you set a tone where ideas and contribution comes from all corners that can positively influence your team and give your company a lead over competitors. Increasingly, the data to support this intuition is being brought to bear and companies are sitting up and listening.

In a January 2015 report, *Diversity Matters* from McKinsey, researchers examined proprietary data sets for 366 public companies across a range of industries in Canada, Latin America, the United Kingdom, and the United States. Simply put, the data showed that diversity helps improve financial results. According to their findings, companies in the top quartile for racial and ethnic diversity are 35 percent more likely to have financial returns above their respective national industry medians. In the United States, there is a linear relationship between racial and ethnic diversity and better financial performance: for every 10 percent increase in racial and ethnic diversity on the senior executive team, earnings before interest and taxes (EBIT) rise 0.8 percent. In the United Kingdom, greater gender diversity on the senior executive team corresponded to the highest performance uplift in the data set: for every 10 percent increase in gender diversity, EBIT rose by 3.5 percent.

In addition to higher performance and increased earnings, there are other reasons to incorporate more diversity in your company culture. With the connectivity and demographic

> **"Being an inclusive workplace is also more important than ever because you won't be able to hide any less-than-stellar practices that your company deploys."**

complexity of the fourth industrial revolution, leaders need to be mindful of the plethora of websites now dedicated to reviewing employers for all manner of practices. If your company is not inclusive, or even accused of counter-inclusive practices, social media will explode with such claims. The best talent will not want to work for a company with such a reputation, and your employees will vote with their feet if they see less than expected behavior by an organization expecting to thrive in this era.

To help develop an inclusive, diverse culture, leaders must hire without prejudice and look for pools of talent that may be underrepresented in their current teams. If your organization is behind the curve on creating an inclusive environment, you might want to start with being honest about how, and from where, you source your talent. If you are hiring from preppy schools in predominantly white areas, you can't be surprised if you don't have a strong community of employees of different racial backgrounds in your company. Get a new list of campuses to recruit from and start calling them. Similarly, make sure you use the technology at your disposal to reach out to a diverse group of candidates in regard to age, race, sex, gender, ethnicity, and social and cultural backgrounds.

Participating in communities where you have not historically engaged will also help you develop a more inclusive culture. Through community events and other outlets that are new to your organization, you can connect with concepts or trends that you may have been less familiar with in the past. As the world changes, so should your approach and attitude—your knowledge base must be progressive. For example, if a conversation about transgender employee rights is starting to permeate the cultural pages of magazines and other news outlets you watch, start educating yourself on the topic. Highlight any weaknesses you have in your knowledge and open yourself up to learning more about issues, concepts, and people that you may not be as familiar with. Don't wait for them to be upon you.

Another positive step toward a more inclusive culture is to look for influencers around your company who can help you link inclusion to innovation and, by doing so, accelerate the entire company's success. Ask them to help you make the mind switch to a more enlightened workplace that reflects the future. For example, you may have a pocket of talent in your organization that has developed a unique way of working together that reflects their diversity. They might work different hours because they are all working parents, or they might use different collaboration methods based on an idea from someone who has worked and lived in another country. If they are getting different and better results, the entire company could likely benefit from their learning, and the rest of their colleagues should hear their example.

No longer is this a world in which people talk about "minorities and majorities." An inclusive workplace reflects the outside world, and you are kidding yourself if you think, "I don't need to deal with that yet" when it comes to societal issues related to race, gender, bias on the basis of one's sexual orientation, age, or more. You have to focus on the shared goals and capabilities of a diverse team needed to succeed, and if you are globally minded and culturally savvy you will be more impactful. Once you have helped direct your team and company toward greater diversity, you can then start focusing on other elements that contribute to the culture.

Team Time Not Face Time

"Face time" has two potential meanings in the context of management and leadership. The first meaning reflects how much time an employee is seen in the office. The second refers to how much time employees have with their leaders or managers in face-to-face meetings. Then of course there is a third definition of FaceTime, the video chat Apple product for iPhone and iPad, which can be a potential solution to solving the woes of the other two meanings.

In regard to developing a company culture, we are speaking about the first definition of face time, in which leaders want their team members to spend time in the same office as their colleagues for the purposes of collaboration, accountability, and coaching. This desire is totally understandable for leaders, especially in the early stage of their leadership journey. There is something that feels "safe" about the ability to see your team come and go, hear the buzz of their work, and have the convenience of tapping someone on the shoulder if you need to ask her something.

We appreciate all of these potential benefits, but if you are a leader building a culture that relies on face time as a core indicator of engagement and productivity, we urge you to make a mind switch *now*. The new world of work renders this view—that face time is a proxy for being "present"—increasingly redundant. Changing demographics and increasing technological developments not only make such an archaic culture less attractive, but they also provide the setting and tools to build a more virtual-minded culture.

Leaders need to focus their energy on time with the team rather than time at the desk. Such a mindset allows them to concentrate on productive and enriching tasks, "meeting" people where they are geographically through technology. There are widely available enterprise social tools that enable teams to collaborate virtually—two examples are Jive and Yammer. Many of the big software players now have an offering that lets employees update the status of projects they are working on, share information efficiently, and build virtual groups within the organization. By staying flexible, face time becomes team time. For many leaders, however, this evolution can be a daunting one—it's hard to adjust to changing ways of communication or interaction.

We admit that if you are from an industry, culture, or demographic where being the first in to the office in the morning, and never leaving before the boss, was viewed as a sign of commitment, then acknowledging that those days are gone will be tough. However, such structured thinking in a tech savvy and diverse workplace can drag down morale and limit your ability to attract and retain talent. The cultural implications of doing away with a face-time leadership style, however, are huge. Not only will this new way of thinking allow you to focus on results as the primary metric for everyone at the company, but it will also be seen as a major benefit to your employees. It allows for those who have long commutes or unusual personal circumstances to contribute without bias or gossip about when they arrived and left the office. (It also limits social distraction at the water cooler.) Naturally there are some work spaces where necessary equipment and operations makes this conversation moot, but increasingly companies are evolving to be service based with humans and automated otherwise, so it is more relevant than ever.

"Seeing someone at a desk is a mental shortcut we use to judge hard work. It simply doesn't apply anymore."

Today, technological advances that have given birth to the remote workforce have made conferencing, connecting, and communicating immeasurably easier. Though we advocate using these remote working tools to enhance your productivity, we also advise that you be careful in how they are implemented: don't let them turn into an invasion of privacy. Numerous companies have discovered firsthand the outrage that can be sparked when seemingly helpful new technologies end up going too far. For example, Britain's *Daily Telegraph* hit the press after monitors were placed under workers' desks. The wireless motion detectors sensed whether employees were using their desks or not, and the company claimed it was monitoring the environment for efficiency reasons (as reported in *The Guardian* and *Buzzfeed* in January 2016). Even if the *Telegraph*'s management had pure intentions, they obviously didn't understand the optics of invading privacy in this way.

MIND SWITCH FACT

A 2015 Gallup poll (Gallup's annual Work and Education poll, conducted August 5–9, 2015) reports that U.S. remote workers have increased in number to 37 percent since 1995 (9 percent of workers). The point is that using face time as a mental shortcut for whether people are doing work is decreasing in effectiveness.

To help develop a culture where "team time" and results are given priority over face time, leaders need to set standards that are both playful and effective. They need to get teams communicating—especially those members who are somewhat unwilling to adapt to change at first. They must also bring levity to the reality that this new world of work, the fourth industrial revolution, exists. In our own experience, this can take time, but the results are indisputable. Kylie once worked with a team whose members had a lot of flexibility in the way they worked. For example, on days they decided to work remotely, they would e-mail their colleagues with the letters "wfc" in the subject line, which meant "working from couch."

> **"Have well-thought-out ideas and an open mind to ask questions to help achieve your goals."**

For Kylie, this process was quite strange to her since she had come from a more face-time culture. Once she got settled in and acclimated, this gesture became charming and liberating. The team was happy, the company was successful, and all was well. Many employees had the freedom to spend their lunchtime or downtime as they saw fit—as long as the leaders were receiving the desired results, there was no need to get bogged down with frivolous meetings or in-person conferences. Debra likes to say that even though she regularly works remotely, she does have an increase of "board" meetings in the summer months—those being days on her stand-up paddleboard.

To get yourself and your team inspired to move away from the traditional face-time culture, reading about companies that have been successful in doing so already can be helpful. JetBlue seems a great example: the company allows its reservations staff to work from home, a factor that led to JetBlue being rated highly by its employees and ranking in the top 20 places to work by *Forbes* in 2015.

Lastly, you should find "hacks"—shortcuts or strategies that allow you to leverage minutes between meetings. An example of a hack might be using voice memos that are texted to your colleagues with follow-ups from the meeting to save you from drafting an e-mail later when your memory has faded. Or perhaps using the customer relationship management (CRM) app on your phone to update a customer profile instead of waiting to get back to your desk later and using the desktop version. Making your accessibility by mobile devices the norm will go a long way to being more efficient, even if you are from a generation that prefers more traditional methods. Landlines are a tether to the past—don't use them unless you have to. Still, you must be aware of the mixed demographics in the work force: age, experience, and technical savvy requires you to ensure that the message sent is heard by all constituents in the manner they need, as well as the platform you prefer.

Of course, all of the newfangled technologies in the world cannot create a productive, positive culture alone. The timeless leadership qualities and behaviors discussed in Part One of the book need to be kept in mind during every step in building your company's or organization's culture. One of the most important ones that we would like to highlight in more detail is that of transparency.

Transparency in the Office

Throughout the book, we've talked about the importance of transparency, especially in regard to the "true blue" leadership quality discussed in Chapter 2. Just like the term "culture" can be tricky, however, so can "transparency." That said, have you ever met someone who wants *less* transparency in a workplace? We certainly haven't. But what "transparency in the workplace" means and what leaders should do to develop a culture of transparency can be entirely different.

The areas of a work environment that usually invite ire around lack of transparency are:

» Compensation
» Executive travel
» Likelihood of corporate takeovers
» Staff departures
» People moving offices or cubicles

These topics are such hot buttons because they touch on the two threads that can be divisive in an organization: the concept of fairness and the idea that executives are secretive because they are living "too high on the hog" or selling out without consulting the masses. While these responses and suspicions are understandable at times, there are usually good reasons that full transparency is hard. Does everyone have a right to know what others earn or what the different pay scales are? Can a company feasibly share likelihood of a takeover without triggering panic and/or rule-breaking by regulators?

Sometimes people raise concern in these areas simply because they feel that they need to be better informed, but at other times, cries for greater transparency can be a signal that there is a breakdown in trust or other similar areas. As a leader you should worry about both.

Some companies believe in sharing everything—from earnings to capital structure, new hires to departures, industry changes to executive policies, and more—so that people can perform their jobs with full context. Other companies use transparency to drive behavior—for example, in an attempt to drive down costs, bosses may expose all employees' expense claims in an attempt to publicly shame certain individuals who overspend. Such decisions are obviously important because they radically change the way people communicate and behave. The underlying belief system for the organization is an important factor in deciding how much, and how far, to share.

By studying companies that believe in a radically transparent culture—one in which leaders and staff members believe in direct and open communication—you can get a sense for the commitment that it entails and form a view on whether it is a good or bad fit for your company's culture. There are some nuances, though, to what topics should be subject to radical transparency. For some companies, radical transparency is about sharing the inner workings of the company, such as sharing all expenses incurred by executives, profits and losses, and so on. For others, it is about communication and sharing positive and negative thoughts and critiques in the spirit of moving the business forward with full information. This second type of transparency is motivated by the removal of politics, back-channel conversations, and information asymmetry.

"Tell no lies nor stretch the truth. Have the confidence to say it like it is. That's good enough."

The path to transparency is technically easier than ever because sharing information is easier than ever. Digital properties of all kinds—off the shelf and custom—give you no excuses on whether or not you have the ability to disseminate pertinent information. As a leader, however, you need to make the choice as to what you need to reveal, and how often. Sharing widely on a continuous basis creates the potential for distraction. When facing hard times, "oversharing" can be a morale kicker to your colleagues, especially if they are unable to directly affect the problem.

When it comes to deciding on the type of culture leaders want to instill, the safest bet to make is that the level of transparency is going to differ slightly at every company or institution, and leaders therefore must be mindful of the context. As a leader working to direct and develop your company's culture, ask yourself:

> "In reality, when we talk about transparency in the workplace we are usually just saying that we want information that others have—not necessarily seeking the higher order goal of clarity."

- » Do you believe there is such a thing as too much information in a workplace?
- » What kind of culture in regard to communicating information currently exists?
- » What topics are sensitive for you and your organization?
- » What will greater transparency achieve for you and your team?
- » Will transparency actually drive better results and/or make people happier?

In our experience, balance in creating a *productive* transparent culture is imperative. Sharing goals, strategy, financials, failures, shifts in thinking, and staff moves is very powerful and, at most times, necessary to succeeding. Sharing confidential processes, tough decisions that are still being made, debt levels, and customer information are more of a gray area and dependent on the specific organization and the ownership structure. For example, public companies have specific reporting requirements that private companies don't, and nonprofits or governments will have their own rules. Intelligence that can be competitively used against you, potentially harm a customer, or give anxiety about the path forward, however, can backfire against you, even when it is shared in the right spirit. With this in mind, great judgment, clarity from leadership about what can and can't be shared, and a willingness to own the outcomes of transparency in rain or shine are crucial to success.

Naturally, even as a leader, you are still part of a team and you will not be the only decision maker on the topic, but you can be a positive force in helping others to understand the power of transparency imbedded in company culture when it is used properly. You should acknowledge that transparency and uber-communication go hand in hand, but are not the same thing. Being transparent doesn't mean oversharing. Listen carefully to your team for their true meaning when they ask for transparency—mostly they are looking for signals that you are trustworthy or they simply want information to do their jobs effectively.

It's also important to use technology thoughtfully in regard to a transparent culture—there are some things that are still best shared behind closed doors. There are also situations that not everyone in a workplace will be equipped to handle if told the full story, so testing messages in a controlled setting first makes sense when you are handling certain types of information. Lastly, avoid being hypocritical on the topic of transparency. To be a trusted leader, you can't expect transparency to be given to you and not to pass it on to others.

Mind Switch on Fostering Company Culture

In the new world of work we have more options than ever to create a productive, inclusive, and transparent culture within our organizations. Technology has given us the gifts we need to succeed, and demographics will force our adoption as the rise of millennials demands a more flexible approach to working styles and interactivity among workers. By using enterprise tools that allow sharing, virtual collaboration, and communication, leaders in the fourth industrial revolution no longer need to rely on mental shortcuts, like physically seeing someone in the office, to do their work effectively. Team time should supplant face time as the mantra within a company with a strong and positive culture. But technology alone can't drive a culture that makes people want to join the organization.

An openness to diversity of thought, inclusive hiring activities (and policies), and a willingness to share the organizational context will all make for a positive "aura" within an organization and reduce distractions that naturally occur when people are anxious or uncertain about how they fit in. More than ever, there are also more diverse stories of successful cultural shifts that showcase enlightened, playful, and uber-communicative leaders. Many of these examples come from the hard-charging Silicon Valley companies, and their global equivalents, but increasingly large and storied companies with rich pasts are embracing new ways to be considered a top place to work for the generations that will dominate the future, as well as those that have engineered success in the past.

STORIES FROM THE ROAD

**Susan Schell, consultant, Business Acumen, LLC,
(www.businessacumenconsulting.com),
writes about mixed generations.**

George was a senior scientist, one of the finest plasma physicists in the world. He worked tirelessly in the lab, experimenting and refining power delivery systems. One of his primary jobs was teaching other engineers a fraction of what he understood after 45 years of work. So much valuable information lived within him and needed to be shared.

But George was not fluent in the language of youth. He did not tweet, blog, pin, Skype, FaceTime, Instagram, or game. In fact, he couldn't even sign in to a conference call or successfully put his phone on hold without asking for help. It was quite a contrast to the dexterity of the youthful employees who spent hours with their mobile devices. George wasn't particularly interested in many of the PC programs either. He had little need for the likes of PowerPoint and Publisher.

The gap was huge. George was part of the "greatest generation"—born just before the baby boomers. He was brilliant and knowledgeable, but set in his ways. His brain was full and not as nimble for learning trendy stuff. Concurrently, the youngest engineers in the plant were late Gen X and early Gen Ys. Although their contemporary educations gave them an edge on new technology and social media, they lacked the experience, connections and insights of their senior partner.

But what seemed like an impossible gap became symbiotic. Baby boomers were inventing the newest and trendiest technology but were selective as users. They were responsible for so much of the evolution of science and nanotechnology. Generation X became a bridge generation. Although they were not raised from birth with technology, they were using it. They also became significant contributors in advancing technology. But finally Generation Y was native and comfortable with all devices and programs. They leaned on George for his brilliance, wisdom, finesse, and maturity. George called upon his youthful teammates for the practical applications of their technology to his work. Since there was mutual respect, it was embraced and beneficial.

These employees spanned four generations. What must be learned from this is that they all make contributions that are valuable, and they all have good intentions. It was not critical in this case for everyone to possess the same skill sets and to labor over the differences. Business cultures can encourage the cross-pollination of multiple generations in the workplace. We must not lose the tribal knowledge by eliminating the elders; nor should we discount the contributions of the fledgling workers.

08

ADDRESSING FEEDBACK AND REWARDS

T he idea of annual reviews strikes fear into the hearts of most white-collar professionals. First and foremost, the prospect of getting unexpected negative ratings is scary. On the flip side, if you are the manager, the idea of giving feedback can be daunting. Whether a high-level manager or an entry-level employee, the sheer time commitment alone can make reviews fear-inducing experiences. According to Charles Rogel of DecisionWise consulting, an average review takes three hours. Adding up the hours invested by managers and employees in this process can lead to a serious financial, as well as emotional, investment. Even if it only takes 30 minutes to write a self-review, or to write one for a team member, in our experience the process seems to paralyze the company for a whole month!

Annual reviews are considered by some (ourselves included) to be flawed because people tend to fall prey to the natural limits of their memories and risk the tendency to overemphasize more recent performance simply because it is fresher in their minds. Employees might have done something outstanding as part of their role in January of one year, but by December (if that is when the annual review is) this has been long forgotten. Frankly, some annual review forms are hastily completed Sunday evening after a day of football and beers to meet a Monday morning deadline. For many people, these reviews are the only point of structured feedback that they get in their professional lives. In our opinion, this lack of regularity is a travesty, and this feedback should not to be taken as factual truth for the whole.

In spite of all the academic studies and consulting rhetoric that you can read, the fact of the matter is that the annual performance review process at most companies still seems to stink. As a leader today, you'll need to overcome poor performance review processes and provide consistent, clear feedback. Your team members need to understand what is expected of them, how they can improve, and what incentives and compensation are tied to their performance.

Managing Performance

Overall, performance management is the tracking, measuring, and communication of an employee's execution of his or her role. Good leaders, however, have a *specific* view on what performance management means to them and the people they work with. Irrespective of their company's stated system for tracking performance, such leaders adopt a positive and regular cadence to monitoring results, giving feedback, and providing guidance—it is the least they can do for those relying on them, and on whom they rely in turn. Numerous theories on what performance management "should be" already exist, and making sense of the many possible meanings has become a key leadership skill.

There are different methodologies and philosophies around performance management, and it is currently a hot topic as the trend toward scrapping the annual review process gains momentum globally. Performance management and the supporting systems and processes is a big spending item for companies, so it absolutely warrants close attention. The estimated size of the market for HR systems alone, including performance management systems, is $10 billion. While the history of performance management can be tracked back to the military, the last few decades of change and evolution are rooted in corporate America with talent-driven companies like GE and McKinsey playing an important role in setting up models for others to follow.

Some leaders and companies still follow the stack ranking methodology popularized by GE and others in the 1980s and sometimes referred to as the "rank and yank" system. The general thrust of the stack ranking system is to bucket people into categories that compare them with the top percentage of performers (e.g., 15 percent), the middle percentage (e.g., 75 percent) and bottom percentage of performers (e.g., 10 percent). These categories are then used to determine the future path for an employee, which, in the most cutthroat deployment of the methodology, means that the bottom percentage are fired. Such numerical ranking of employees has had many different iterations over time, and their benefits are that they force structure and, theoretically at least, an objective system to measure and compare performances.

We worked with a leader for many years who was more passionate about performance management, including a numerical ranking system of measurement, than almost any other aspect of his responsibilities. At year's end, he would read every review written by his direct reports and become furious if they lacked detail, objectivity, data, or sufficient constructive criticism. We can still remember him unleashing his temper over poorly executed reviews. It had a huge impact on us—a very positive one. It seemed fair of him to ask: if you can't pour your energy into an annual review and have sufficient data, anecdotal evidence, and input from others, are you really leading people? He made this point emphatically.

Considering the contemporary multicultural and multigenerational workforce, you can't go into performance reviews at the end of year and use the same approach with everyone. Increasingly though, performance management systems that are designed around reviewing past performance and using structured time frames tied to a calendar (such as annual reviews) are becoming less popular. The reasoning is that business cycles are now more fluid than in the past and the heavy emphasis on past performance is not healthy for a dynamic organization. We think this is a positive change given the new world of work where technology development and demographic diversity open opportunities for better-than-ever tools and ideas around how to get the best out of your people.

The need for leaders to customize their performance management to generation and style cannot be overemphasized.

This goes for both giving and receiving performance reviews. For example, people from a command and control past will be less comfortable with a performance management conversation that is two-way and will likely want more unilateral communication. A leader who works in a creative and collaborative environment, however, may find it challenging to give directions that are clear and unambiguous in a performance management setting. Yet this kind of agility—to be directive when necessary and two-way when needed—is critical for the fourth revolution leader, embodying the idea of dynamic leadership discussed in Part One.

To help yourself stay agile in the performance management process, you should first build a personal board of advisors that have experience in this regard. Ask their views on how to get the best out of people using performance management. Human resources professionals can also be a useful source of expertise on best practices, case studies, legal and regulatory implications of performance management and actions, and in sharing the company's formal philosophy. That said, the HR team has a complicated role to play in performance management as they need to represent leadership, be an advocate for employees, and be an effective business partner to line managers. Wearing all of these hats at once is not easy!

"I'm currently trying to develop two aspects of leadership— helping those that I manage achieve their dreams/realize their passions and managing process/ organizational change."

Irrespective of the regularity or process your organization uses, make sure to never reschedule a performance management conversation. This very simply tactic will signal the importance of these meetings to your team members.

Unfortunately, many managers fail on this front because they become too busy or overscheduled. If you schedule the meeting, have it, unless unique circumstances, such as a death or something equally dire, arise.

In any performance management meeting, always document the conversation to follow up on potential opportunities discussed or development suggestions made. Sharing that documentation will allow for alignment or readjustment after the fact if the message you gave or received was not the same as intended.

Most important, reconsider the people and performance management functions at your company or organization—it may be time for a total overhaul. For example, in 2015 Accenture was one of the first movers in what has now become a significant shift in thinking on annual performance reviews by large companies. Accenture abandoned them altogether and is reportedly changing up to 90 percent of its talent practices. In the words of its CEO, Pierre Nanterme, "We're going to evaluate you in your role, not vis à vis someone else who might work in Washington, who might work in Bangalore. It's irrelevant. It should be about you." Other companies have followed suit: GE is apparently revolutionizing the way it evaluates its talent using an app called PD@GE (professional development at GE) as a central piece of an ongoing feedback strategy. The app is reportedly used for storing notes on progress toward priorities and for getting feedback in an efficient way.

> **"The trend is definitely for more regular and less cumbersome methods of evaluation and feedback."**

Having a view on how you evaluate your direct reports and contribute to others' performance management through 360 degree reviews—where peers, managers, and direct reports provide commentary on your performance—and direct feedback is crucial to the dynamic you build in a team and your ability to get results. Ongoing performance conversations and a true passion for each person's individual development should be the goal. This process begins with regular, clear, and specific feedback.

Creating Alignment Through Regular Feedback

The simple act of giving employees feedback leads to a closer understanding of the alignment between a leader's expectations and the reality of what is getting done. This is what makes feedback powerful: it can break down misunderstandings and accelerate alignment on where a team or company should be going and how to get there. Whether through compliments, redirections, clarifications, or straight-up praise, leaders should be both positive and constructive in the process—although when people ask for feedback, you can comfortably guess that they prefer praise over anything else!

Giving feedback is a great way to establish trust with your team and peers. It shows that you care about them and their performance, even if their defenses are raised or they are surprised by your candor. Ensuring people that you are sharing feedback because you want mutual success is one of the hardest parts of becoming a leader. Remember, though, you are only trying to help these individuals, and your company, improve. If you are consistent and fair, over time, most people will recognize this, even if you dish out some "tough love" occasionally.

Providing feedback is also an essential way for a great coach to develop leaders for the future. Many employees will be thankful for the opportunity to learn more and willing to implement your suggestions. In fact, according to a TriNet study reported in *Fast Company*, 85 percent of NetGens would feel more confident if they could have more frequent conversations with their managers. (The TriNet Perform Survey was conducted by Wakefield Research [www.wakefield research.com] between September 4–15, 2015, among 1,000 U.S. fulltime employees born after 1980, using an e-mail invitation and an online survey. This survey has a margin of error of +/- 3.1 percentage points.) This is a staggeringly high percentage. Greater confidence will inspire these employees to reach for higher goals, and attain them, while also priming them for leadership roles down the line.

Getting feedback on your own performance can also build trust with your team and help you improve as a manager and leader. Just as you should be regularly giving feedback to others, you should be consistently receiving feedback as well. The same rules apply for leaders as employees: be open to others' suggestions and view feedback as a learning experience and chance for development.

> "Good phrases to use: 'You did uncommonly well.' 'You're the best.' 'You're a genius.' 'You never let me down.' Said only if it's true. And don't overdo it as it dilutes it. If you give daily praise, the day you forget becomes a problem."

As with many topics discussed throughout the book, feedback is easier than ever to give and get today. All aspects of your life are now wired to give you real-time signals. Everything from our Fitbit wearable device to the plethora of emoticons that people send us each day gives us feedback of sorts. But real, human interaction is still important.

Online tools are everywhere for real-time feedback, but face-to-face delivery remains ever powerful and effective.

Nuances can be lost if you overuse digital mechanisms, and today's leaders know that the human touch is necessary to motivating and mentoring their teams.

The Art of Giving Feedback

Make no mistake: there is an art to giving feedback that takes time and practice. Something as simple as giving a compliment can go wrong if the timing, place, or relationship with the person you are complimenting isn't right. The basic rules to providing feedback are to give constructive redirections in private and positive feedback more publicly (though make sure the recipient is not going to be embarrassed). Always give feedback

> **"Be the same to my face as you are behind my back."**

close to the activity that sparked it—nine months after the fact won't be helpful, especially not if it is constructive feedback.

Some leaders prefer the "sandwich" style of delivering feedback: first they give a positive point, then a constructive point, then another positive point. This process will boost employees' confidence while also showing them where they can improve. Leaders can also simply share their criticisms or praise in order of priority. And, of course, sometimes it may be possible to apply only one type of feedback over another. The most important thing is to share it regularly and make it memorable.

The most memorable feedback Kylie ever received in her career came at a time when she was rising quickly through different roles in a company and being challenged in new ways. Her boss gave her feedback during a one-on-one meeting that her verbal communication skills were lacking. She was totally shocked. As a confident presenter and interactive leader, she had always been praised for her ability to communicate clearly. His point, however, was that as you gain success, the bar for communication skills moves. If you want to be able to present to a board or influence a tough group of peers, a different style and strength is required. It was a pivotal point for her career—she regrouped, practiced, and moved onward with his help.

To provide usable, productive feedback, leaders must tie it to specific company or team goals and values. For example, start the conversation by discussing the context of the goal that you are trying to achieve. If you are trying to hit a companywide sales goal and employees do not understand the importance of their individual contribution, provide this detail to help them see the bigger picture. Next, make sure to relate the feedback you provide to how the goal is, or is not, being met. Try to clear your mind before giving feedback and focus on the goal of the feedback—never make it personal. Even in Kylie's situation, the goal was to help her improve her communication skills, not just tell her that she was lacking in some way.

> **"Don't wait until the review to tell people you appreciate their work or help them get better."**

Leaders must also use multiple methods of giving positive feedback. For example, leaders can text employees at the end of a meeting if they were particularly additive to the conversation. Or they could cc an employee on an e-mail to a higher-up, showing that they are crediting her for her great work. As a leader, consider calling your team members, as compared to e-mailing them, to say how much you appreciated something they did. Simply leaving a sticky note on an employee's desk to say "well done" can go a long way. Being uber-communicative is a hallmark of the fourth revolution leader in waiting.

Ask yourself if you have provided feedback to three different people you work with this week. If not, you are losing opportunities to make your product, service, team, or organization better.

Rewarding Performance Through Compensation

No matter how leaders provide feedback or conduct overall performance management, they must set out clear goals for their employees on how performance appraisals relate to compensation. Compensation is simply the way leaders reward paid work, stemming directly from the results of an employee's tasks, duties, and responsibilities. However, there are a complex mix of views around the amount, frequency, and delivery method of compensation that only good leaders know how to handle deftly. Compensation can come in different forms and money is not a universal motivator. Being "compensated" could be rewarded in time off, access to the newest technology, special training and education, a free health club membership, or even a note to an employee's mother about the stellar person she raised.

As a leader, one of the core skills you will need to develop is the ability to be objective. This is especially important when it comes to handling this confidential and sensitive topic—there is barely a more emotional one for those on the receiving end of the compensation conversation. Being able to deftly communicate compensation terms in the hiring, evaluation, promotion, and performance management processes is part of the mastery of the leadership tool kit. An important evolutionary step for managers to make on their journey to leadership is learning not to project their own views on others. For example, if you are anxious about hav-

"Be humble and grounded enough to know that growth takes time and an open mind."

ing compensation conversations with your own boss, you can't let that interfere with the way you lead compensation conversations with your direct reports. Instead, you need to form a view centered on how to get results in any situation as a key leadership skill.

Even if you aren't at the level of your company where you get to determine your reward system, including compensation and benefits, the way you think about it and handle questions on money can mean the difference between inspiring and demotivating those around you. As a leader, it is only a matter of time before you receive these questions during performance reviews and other meetings with your employees:

» "How can I earn more?"
» "How is my bonus determined?"
» "When will I get a pay raise?"
» "Why do other people on the team earn more than me?"

There is only one certainty when it comes to compensation conversations: it will be a rare situation when the majority of people on staff are happy with the outcomes. It is human nature to compare yourself with others and feel restless if the most quantifiable value of your output might be less than you think it should be (or that others around you might be getting more than they should be!). This is a timeless dilemma for both managers and individuals alike.

Money conversations can be particularly treacherous for the new manager. To be trusted with compensation decisions and delivery, leaders not only need to be objective, but they must have great dexterity around unexpected employee reactions—they are a certainty. This is especially true in today's environment of rapid change. Just as the backgrounds of your team and the diversity of their experiences will affect how you provide performance reviews and feedback, they will also make for a widely varied set of expectations around how much and by what method people get paid. For some people, stability is all that matters. For others, the sense of being able to make more money if they perform better than expected, through variable compensation, or having other "skin in the game," such as shares in the company they work for, are important drivers in their satisfaction with the rewards of the job.

Even if you are not at the point in your career where you decide on others' compensation, you should start forming your views now. Ask yourself:

» Do you believe in pay-for-performance systems where incentives are generally aligned to the business strategy and success?

» Do you like discretion in setting bonuses, or do you prefer them to be algorithmically determined?

» Do you think equitable pay is more important than rewarding high performers by paying them more than lower performers, despite job title, length in the role, or status?

» Do you think more pay drives better performance or just builds a competitive environment where people are pitted against each other?

» Do you think merit-based pay systems, where individual performance can be rewarded separate from overall business performance, is the way to keep your best people?

MIND SWITCH FACT

In a 2015 PayScale study of more than 5,000 businesses, researchers found that 63 percent of employers cited "retaining top employees" as their primary compensation objective. However, 57 percent do not train managers how to speak with employees about compensation, and 38 percent are not very confident in their managers' ability to perform this task.

These questions are all big ones for a rising leader, especially since what worked in the past regarding compensation may not work today.

Leaders need to keep reviewing their teams' expectations, and checking for whether they are reasonable and/or sufficiently aspirational, reviewing data, and always looking outside their own companies to see what others in the market and different industries are doing—if other organizations are offering better compensation in some way, you'll lose your best people to them. It's therefore imperative to stay on top of the trends.

To increase the complication, what attracts people to your company may be very different from what retains them, and *that* may be very different from what makes them leave. Motivations to work for you in the fourth industrial revolution, with such a mixed workforce, will look very different than in the past. It will look even more so in the future once Gen Z becomes a powerful force. In the words of Australian teenager Nick D'Aloisio, who sold his news aggregation app to Yahoo for $30 million: "We are so young, the success I've had isn't a cause of jealousy or envy. It's almost abstract. Money is one way of equating success but the way I like to equate it is: how far are you willing to take your interests and pursue them, or just how well rounded are you as an individual? Do you live in a meaningful way, do you have everything together?" Taking this type of mindset into consideration may lead you to rethink how your team or company handles performance-based compensation with younger generations. Your company may even consider retooling the entire compensation structure.

Given the sensitivity of compensation conversations and processes, however, companies are often loath to make sweeping changes. They opt instead for constant tweaks, which can be frustrating and confusing for their teams. In 2015, there was an interesting case related to this compensation dilemma when the CEO of a little-known Seattle-based company called Gravity Payments increased the base salary for everyone in the company to $70,000. The average salary was previously $48,000, so many people got big pay raises. (https://www.nytimes.com/2015/04/14/business/owner-of-gravity-payments-a-credit-card-processor-is-setting-a-new-minimum-wage-70000-a-year.html) The CEO's motivation was reported as a desire to increase happiness by taking away financial stress for the lowest paid employees. The story became a national conversation with 500 million interactions on social media almost immediately. But of course not everyone at this company was happy. Some people left because they thought the move was a bad sign. One team member who left said the change essentially "shackle[d] high performers to less motivated team members." Point being, even when leaders try to make the right decisions, the complexity of compensation can lead to surprising, and sometimes negative, results.

The Power of Compensation

Despite the complexity of compensation decisions and communication, they can be powerful levers when leaders are trying to drive change, stimulate growth, or send a specific message about a desired or undesirable behavior. Some leaders believe it is *the* most powerful way to do so, and there is a deep body of academic work dedicated to this area. Our experience has been mixed. It is most clear that compensation is a powerful lever for sales teams. Once you move into other technical or service fields, the path for how to use compensation to drive behavior becomes less clear—the importance of how deftly you handle it remains constant. Thriving in such an environment takes enlightened leaders who know their companies are competing for attention with the most formidable opponents to hire and keep the best talent.

Understanding these drivers for your key team members and most valuable talent is your best defense against finding yourself surprised when someone decides to leave. This means that receiving feedback from your team on a regular basis is paramount to success. Having your finger on the pulse of employee sentiment, attitude, and general contentment at work will better help you judge how to

> **"Money is simply one lever they have; there are many other drivers that also matter now."**

keep your team together and productive. In some ways, compensation is the most complicated to get right but the clearest and most quantifiable (and comparable) of all the factors that go into attracting good people. It is therefore important to master the communication around it, which only comes with confidence in your views and much practice.

One way to begin developing skills around handling compensation questions and conversations is to practice with a HR partner. This is crucial in a leader's learning experience and development. Always knowing the precise dollar amounts that are to be distributed to an individual is the first hurdle to clear—communicating them accurately and crisply is the next.

Make no assumptions about your team member when going into conversations or performance reviews that could potentially touch on the topic of compensation. You may be surprised to find that not everyone will care as much as the next person about monetary rewards, but a team member may want some other type of compensation (e.g., more time off or greater flexibility in his schedule). Simply put, let your team tell you what matters most to them in driving great performance.

Lastly, you should never, ever, change the timing or amount of compensation without a detailed in-person conversation first. Text is not an appropriate way to communicate on this topic. More important, being trustworthy is behavior number one in this area.

The Mind Switch on Feedback and Rewards

People don't only work for a "company," they work for an individual manager, and that manager has the power and the responsibility to help her people grow. Leaders make leaders out of others. A good manager and boss wants to be as smart as she can be and wants her people to be, too. That requires specific feedback addressed without criticism or judgment of character or motive or ability—only behavior. A good leader protects her people from emotional strife by making clear, "This is what I want, and this is what I don't want" and "Here is how you will be compensated." Never fail to smile and be consistently, unfailingly pleasant up and down the ladder. The leader has to educate what is going to, and needs to be done with considerate civility, so as to build a team.

STORIES FROM THE ROAD

Kristi Riordan, COO at the Flatiron School, writes about communicating across teams in times of high growth.

Founded in 2012 and headquartered in lower Manhattan, the-Flatiron School is a venture-backed company providing web and mobile development courses to adults seeking a new career. I joined as COO to help build the foundation for future growth.

About one year into our Series A financing round, we began to notice increasing challenges with our internal communication. We would address issues as they arose, but it seemed that we were constantly reactive and addressing similar problems with increasing cost—especially the faster we grew. I learned, maybe the hard way, that communication is the fuel of a growth organization—and it can either create high velocity teams, or slow everything down to a halt.

At the time, we were successfully running a stable service product with one team, developing a software product with a second team, and scaling a product with a third team when we started to feel the costs of growth on our employee morale. As a leadership team, we were focused primarily on the everyday stresses of operations, and we couldn't have been more excited for our prospects. But it eventually became apparent that not everyone shared our outlook. Concerns began reverberating around the organization, unnerving some of our staff, and quickly we had a serious company morale problem—despite the fact that we had great business prospects and great opportunities for employees to move up and take on greater responsibility. Not fully understanding the root cause of the discontent, I began a series of one-on-one conversations across the organization. Despite the apparent resilience in many areas, some of my conversations painted a picture of dire straits across the entire company. During my listening tour I did not try to persuade anyone. I asked a lot of questions and tried to listen carefully.

The effects of our rapid growth were both uneven and unpredictable—while some parts of the company seemed to feel that things were breaking down, other teams were thrilled by the challenges of a nimble business strategy. Each product team needed something slightly different—but one thing was consistent. While the organization was changing rapidly, our communication wasn't keeping up to connect employees to each other and keep them informed of our broader strategy.

Employees who didn't have the context or organizational perspective to see the need for the changes were sometimes bewildered. Candidly, some people had an individual interest that no longer aligned with the company strategy. That situation will never be easy, but it's fair to say we hadn't done everything we might have to draw that to a healthy conclusion. Some people were excited about what our current strategy might hold for them but felt disconnected, confused, and exhausted. The largest group of people were engaged and doing just fine, but the concern of other employees was reverberating across the company and beginning to shift our overall morale. Almost everyone I spoke with had strong emotions about our business and their relationship to it. It became increasingly clear to me that company morale was not just a human resources issue—it was one of the most powerful assets we had to either accelerate or slow our business growth.

Interestingly enough, Flatiron School's primary business provides students a 12-week immersive coding class that includes nearly 800 hours of training. This program has a huge learning curve for students with a structured growth cycle that we had repeated many times, making it easy to recognize a pattern. Students would come in with excitement and feel invigorated by the program. Within just a few weeks, our instructors would introduce complicated material, sending many students spiraling into feelings of frustration and panic, to the point that many feared they were not cut out to be programmers. We saw this pattern repeat across every class, with every type of student, every semester.

After watching several student terms, I realized the disruptive pattern caused by growth was quite similar to what happens to employees within business growth. Further, I realized that growth cycles were easier (*while still hard*) for me because I had some perspective from past cycles. Many of our employees were facing their first growth cycles and did not have that perspective to self-diagnose, work through issues, and be able to see around the curve.

Taking inspiration from our educators, I set out to normalize some of the feelings that occur during the more challenging phases of growth. I focused on isolating the emotions I saw when we were engaged and at our best, as well as fraying at the edges. I began to refer to them as driver (high velocity) and dragger (low velocity) emotions. I talked about the fact that we all cycle through these emotions. I wanted to encourage self-diagnosis and a team that would work together to navigate us back to our driver states.

We experience many feelings during growth: Drivers are:

» Happiness
» Confidence
» Energy
» Calmness
» Collaboration
» Clarity

Draggers are:

» Frustration
» Fear
» Exhaustion
» Panic
» Isolation
» Confusion

I was convinced that if we did a better job of recognizing our own emotions and those of the people around us, they might serve as a leading indicator of problems within the company, giving us an opportunity to address issues early. In hindsight, I could see there had been periods when we had let "dragger" emotions linger for too long without addressing the underlying problem, and we had allowed small problems to become much bigger than they really were.

Related to this, I found that our ability to communicate effectively would often deteriorate with the internal draggers (stressors) we might be feeling through a particular growth phase. Good communication is a stimulant. It's the difference between walking out of a meeting energized by what lay before us—or one where we feel frustrated, disengaged, and confused. I then began to similarly categorize communication patterns where I saw our staff in a driver (high velocity) and dragger (low velocity) state.

And how can our communication affect our velocity? Drivers are:

» Solution-oriented
» Inquisitive and listening
» Inviting and patient
» Celebratory; affirming and acknowledging

Draggers are:

» Problem-oriented
» Declarative and telling
» Aggressive and escalating
» Shaming (sarcastic); condescending and dismissive

This entire process helped me realize that emotions are the engine of a growth organization and communication is the fuel. If we wanted to go anywhere, we had to be able to cycle through the stresses of growing a company and get back to our driver states. And, we needed to find a way to do this proactively.

Today, our leadership team continues to look for ways to communicate in a very agile way. Some of the tactics we have initiated include:

» Quarterly company meetings—includes formal presentations on our mission, vision, strategy, goals, progress, and other current company issues.

» A weekly internal newsletter—includes more granular and data-driven updates around the company from the past week and acknowledges employee contributions.

» A weekly all hands meeting—a more informal in-person meeting with open Q&A and shout-outs to teammates.

» Small group leadership lunches—one member of our leadership team will have lunch with a handful of employees to encourage more candid Q&A and build cross-functional relationships.

Across the company, we work to encourage individual agency to spot problems and develop solutions:

» New hire training program—includes a session on "Operating in a Growth Environment" where we describe the common cycles of growth and related feelings.

» Regular feedback cycles—a structured weekly (or biweekly) one-on-one meeting to ensure feedback is regularly collected and can be addressed early.

In a rapidly growing company, it can be very difficult to keep employees informed of shifting strategies in a way that confirms they are a valued part of the effort. Since we began devoting more resources to communicating with employees and developing our diagnostic framework, we've become faster at spotting potential problems and exploiting opportunities. But the pursuit of great communication is never ending.

«‹›»

Sharon Clinebell, professor of management and director of Daniels Fund Ethics Initiative at the Monfort College of Business, University of Northern Colorado, writes about changing attitudes.

As a longtime professor, I see students' behavior change with the generational changes. The presence of helicopter parents is well known in academic circles. I gave a student an F for a paper that was largely plagiarized from the book. Plagiarism had been explained to students, and they were told that their grade would be very negatively impacted if I detected plagiarism. I was also incredulous that he plagiarized right out of the book, which was very easy for me to catch. The next day after returning the papers, I received a phone call from his father. His father was very nice and very contrite. The student's parents had written his paper for him, and they did not realize that what they did was plagiarism. As the conversation evolved, I found out that the parents were at their wit's end with their son. They had spent a lot of money, which I gathered was quite a sacrifice for them, on his college education. Throughout his college career, he was a poor student who sometimes failed classes because he was not submitting homework or papers. He was in his fifth year, and the parents could not afford to continue paying tuition, so they starting doing his homework for him.

Millennial students are well known for their dependence on and closeness to their parents. A concern is that students are not developing autonomy and, in this case, the student was taking advantage of his parents.

I don't really know the result of this story. The F on the paper stood, and I cannot remember what grade he received in the class. I have wondered if the student graduated. With his poor work ethic, I cannot see him being very successful unless he finally matured. I felt very sorry for the parents. They desperately wanted their son to have a college degree, which they did not have. They wanted to provide a better life for their son, but in doing so, they were enabling him to be a failure.

09

PRIORITIZING DECISIONS

Though it may sound trite, during your career as a leader, there will be a moment in which you suddenly realize that time is finite. The youthful version of yourself will struggle with time management, overcommitting to tasks and responsibilities as you try to get ahead. No one, however, likes to work for, or with, harried and overstretched leaders whose schedules are so jam-packed that they are unavailable outside of structured weekly meetings or mandatory "check-ins." And we would argue that nobody starts out wanting to be that kind of leader.

You will be faced with the constant challenge of prioritizing what is most important to help your team and company succeed. Sometimes, it's hard to tell what those priorities are, but decision making is a leader's inescapable responsibility, so you will be the one who has to decide. If you don't make up your mind, someone else will do it for you. Indecisiveness will give others the power to be in charge of your actions, career, even life, and who wants that?

In the prioritization process, you must learn to let go and delegate work to others, while motivating and leading them toward the desired results. Staying decisive and keeping your employees engaged can be tough, but once you're able to do so, you'll find that the whole team will function more smoothly, hit planned targets, and achieve overall success.

The Prioritization Process

Before the tech revolution, people's work lives used to be simpler and more straightforward. If you were an office worker, you prioritized your activities by your physical inbox, the time that the mail delivery occurred, or the sequence of phone calls that you received that day. Today, people are constantly bombarded by Outlook meeting requests, e-mails, text messages, social media updates, and a plethora of never-ending data and intelligence that they need to incorporate into their thinking. Yet in a day where you have more apps to manage your time than days in the year, and your devices buzz and ping all day reminding you of the tasks you are meant to do, it can be challenging to actually get *anything* done. Choosing which activities to complete in this environment is confusing at best.

In any given day, you have activities that you could do, want to do, hate to do, and/or need to do. Prioritization is all about getting results with the shortest yet most elegant path possible—it is also perhaps the hardest of all leadership challenges. The truth is that "getting results" can be interpreted in 900 different ways. You must therefore first decide how *you* define "results." Consider these questions:

>> **Are results the same as metrics for you?** Metrics are generally objective measures of the output of an activity. Results could imply a broader view that encompasses impacts that are harder to measure quantitatively. For example, the result of a specific sales initiative might lead to new revenue, but it might also provide an innovative solution that helps the product team to develop a new source of revenue for the future. The results are more positive than the new revenue implies.

>> **Do you think of results in purely financial terms?** If you are the kind of leader that thinks the end game is a financial result and everything else is "fluff," then you need to be clear about that with your team at the outset of any activity.

>> **Do you believe in giving guidance on how to arrive at the results you want, or is initiative and creativity part of the result that you want?** In some industries, creativity and initiative is crucial to the process of getting a good result—for example, advertising or film production. But in others, strong guidance on how to get to the result and strict adherence to the instructions is part of getting a good result—for example, industries where safety requires strict protocols.

>> **Do you require results within ethical boundaries, and if so, what are they?** The output of some roles is more easily measured than for others. If you are leading a sales team, there may be a temptation to set numerical results and just drive toward those

numbers. However, if there are ethical boundaries—
for example, not calling certain people or respecting
other salespeople's territories—then those need to be
integrated into your definition of results.

» **Are results to be met at any cost or only if the long-
term ramifications are positive?** This question gets at
the heart of long-term and short-term trade-offs. Companies have long-term strategies, and some leaders
make the mistake of celebrating short-term results that
later hurt the business—for example, an aggressive
outreach plan to sell a new product ultimately hurts
the brand because customers are intimidated by the
overly pushy approach taken.

These questions are all branches of the same tree, but each
has a slightly different texture and depth. Answering each
of them is important to understanding what "results" mean
to you before you discuss them with your peers, colleagues,
and direct reports. After defining the concept of "results,"
you must then find a way to achieve them through prioritizing your daily individual or team actions. In addition to
ranking day-to-day activities, you must also consider the
long-range, or long-term, projects that need attention. Some
time each day should be carved out for such activities—don't
let them be ignored.

MIND SWITCH FACT

Global management consultant McKinsey conducted a
study in 2013 that asked nearly 1,500 executives across
the globe to tell them how they spent their time. "Only

> 52 percent said that the way they spent their time largely matched their organizations' strategic priorities."

A simple but effective way to rank the importance and order of performing a certain activity or function is to consider (a) whether you are the only one that could or should perform it or (b) if the action has the likelihood of impacting results in the medium term. Using a 1-to-5 scaling system—1 as most important and 5 as least important—for part (b) of this ranking exercise gives you enough latitude to make incremental judgments without overcomplicating the situation. Ranking your activities by whether you are the only one that should or could do them, and how impactful they will be, will help you create two paths: delegation (if someone else could or should do them) or execution (if they are going to impact results). Execution is straightforward—you personally need to take action. Delegation, however, can be tricky.

Delegation

At its most basic core, "delegation" is the act of a leader assigning tasks to others. It seems like a simple concept, but to be successful leaders need to create a balance between freeing up their own time to focus on other demands and keeping an eye on their employees who are performing the tasks. Leaders must delegate prime opportunities to their best people, which will help these employees or colleagues develop into leaders themselves over time.

When deciding how to delegate responsibilities, the first question to ask yourself is what type of leader are you at your most extreme? Are you an "autocrat" or a "laissez-faire" leader? Do you like giving directives and keeping tight control on the process, or do you prefer explaining the goal and letting others take charge? There are good and bad side effects of both styles, but knowing which one you favor is important to unlocking how realistic it will be for you to delegate effectively.

Laissez-faire leaders are also commonly called "hands-off," and most of us either love 'em or hate 'em. It can be incredibly liberating to work for laissez-faire leaders because they give you space and trust you to make the right decisions. But as Kylie (a self-confessed hands-off leader) likes to often quote to her team, "You live by the sword and die by the sword"—with great trust comes great responsibility. Laissez-faire leaders tend toward communicating the end point of a project or initiative and then leaving a lot of leeway as to how it is achieved. They trust but verify along the way rather than questioning or directing constantly. This gives people a sense of freedom, but if things don't work out on that project or initiative, then consequences can be harsh.

On the flip side, the autocrats basically break out in hives at the idea of handing activities off to others without very specific accountability, requests for updates, regular metrics, and instructions on methodology to be followed. In the delegation process, however, leaders must let go of the idea that they can *always* do something more effectively than someone else. Let's face it: we are all replaceable! As a leader, you must learn to take a step back. If you are worried about the results, and what leader wouldn't be, make sure to first discuss the task with a trusted team member before you move on to more of your own strategic work. (This is the "aha" stage of delegation.)

MIND SWITCH FACT

Forty-five percent of U.K. entrepreneurs participating in a study on delegation completed by the British Telegraph and Omnicom Media, Entrepreneurial Britain, found it difficult to delegate.

(http://www.telegraph.co.uk/connect/small-business/
business-support/is-delegation-the-answer-to-burnout/)

There are industries and leadership roles where each of these leadership delegation styles is more applicable, but there are also generational trends that we need to be mindful of as we develop our own style for the future. Keep in mind, delegation is a skill that requires a lot of mutual respect between bosses and their employees.

With the texture of the workplace having dramatically changed, some generations are just less comfortable with strictly imposed delegation of tasks and duties. Though it may be a generalization, there is a greater unwillingness today from Gen X and Gen Z members to be delegated to, due to the sense of freedom that they have come to recognize and desire. They have grown up in a time when their peers' start up companies in high school and the cost of entry into a business can be boiled down to a laptop and an innovative idea.

> "When you are the one delegated to, do more than expected, more than asked. Don't require lots of reminders to complete assignments."

No matter the makeup of the workforce, the power to delegate is integral to a leader's success. Once you understand how to prioritize tasks most effectively, you can then outline two paths for every item on your "to-do" list: one path is to do it yourself, and the second is to delegate. Imagine all the time you could reclaim to be personally more productive while also empowering others—this is delegation at its best. Embrace the idea that the process is not only about freeing up your time, but also about making more leaders. This will orient you toward sharing credit and elevating the people who help you do your job well. Remember, delegation is not about power or superiority.

We go so far as to say that you should also delegate the "sexiest" aspects of your work when you can, but not the riskiest. There is a big difference between the two. For example, if there is an international travel opportunity where one of your team members could benefit more from the experience than you, or an analysis that your junior employees could perform to give them unique opportunities to work on the company strategy, then pass the reins along to them. The riskiest work requires more finesse and experience—for example, where external parties are involved, where the project is controversial, or where a lot of influence is needed to succeed. Either way, take responsibility for the outcome if it is a failure. If it is a success, give all the glory to your team members.

> **"Delegation is *not* all about offloading stuff you don't like doing."**

When delegating, make sure to describe any task face-to-face with the people you have in mind to see if they have genuine interest in taking it on. Then follow up in writing, setting expectations around deliverables and timing of completion. Calendarize check-in points to make sure they are proceeding as you expected and that success will follow. In delegating work and explaining priorities to others, uber-communication is key.

Communicating Priorities

A major hurdle to prioritization is communicating to a team what tasks or activities must take precedence in a clear and consistent way. You want to make sure that there is no chance of your employees or colleagues misinterpreting the importance of the activities that will drive the best results. You need to be repetitive when sharing these desired results and outcomes. Share them in person, by e-mail, in a drawing on the wall, and even in your social media. At first, you will feel like a broken record, but it will pay off over time.

Regularly referencing results—in numbers and relative to goals—in your conversations will provide context for why people are performing certain actions, tasks, functions, or jobs. These reminders will also maintain clarity on the reasons behind your requests, keep your audience and you honest, and signal to others that you are a serious leader that cares both about your people and about the success of the enterprise. In addition to in-person conversations, it is important to utilize the technology options at your disposal, organizing and calendarizing activities once you have ranked them and then communicating these priorities to all involved. Using a weekly update e-mail or quarterly town hall meeting to review priorities publicly will also help ensure that everyone is on the same page and knows what needs to get done to reach the set goals.

It is also imperative that leaders contextualize priorities to their teams to help make the likelihood of results real and present. This means setting the backdrop as well as the practicality. For example, leaders must give direct, specific information: "If our team is going to hit the

"You owe it to them as a leader to make the end goal clear and constantly reminded. It will help motivate them toward the cause. "

target of $100 in revenue, we will need to sell 10 units at $10 each by the end of next week." While leaders might have different subgoals each year, there should be a measure of success that is consistent year in year out, something that results can be measured against on a regular and timely basis. For example, if we meet our goals as a team, we will hit our company growth rates, which are expected to be more than 10 percent each year.

> **"This is hard in a world where distractions are endless— interruptions come from our devices, our wearables, our environment, and other humans."**

In a fluid workplace, people are coming and going, the gig economy phenomenon is accelerating, and the idea of sitting in one role for a long time is history. They are distracted by their many responsibilities, uncertain what should take precedence, and probably all have different views on how much, or which, results matter. Getting employees to care about these results as much as you do, and sharing your vision for attaining them, will be your communication challenge. Inherent in this challenge is your ability to motivate your teams and employees to actually attain these goals.

Motivating Your Teams and Employees

The way you motivate your best talent toward a common goal or desired result will define you as a leader in the long term. As mentioned earlier in the book, using the bimodal "carrot or stick" motivation method won't work in the future. That method implies that people only care about reward *or* punishment. Increasingly that paradigm has shifted as the concepts of working with a mission and "doing well by doing good" matters more than monetary rewards to some members of the workforce, especially as the millennial generation increases their footprint on it.

The use of carrot *and* stick is a more useful rubric but still doesn't cover the spectrum of choices to motivate and reward a team. This way of motivating—in which leaders simply rewarded or punished—may have worked in the 1990s, but a more personalized approach to managing and leading is necessary in the fourth industrial revolution. Top talent today will be looking for a more contemporary and relatable solution.

Theorists on the topic of motivation talk about "extrinsic" and "intrinsic" motivators. Extrinsic motivation focuses on external factors or rewards, such as monetary compensation, while intrinsic motivation refers to internal rewards, such as the satisfaction of interesting and challenging work or increasing responsibility. Today, there is more of

> "The answers don't come from the top anymore, they come from everywhere."

an emphasis on intrinsic motivation than ever before; mission and culture matter deeply to employees and may be more important than a large salary or big end-of-year bonus.

Most important, as a leader, people above, below, and around you will be motivated by a various array of activities and rewards. They will assess their career options differently than in the past and question their happiness at work more frequently. For example, in the second industrial revolution (the era of cars and machines), the thought of leaving one's job because the technology was lagging or the hours were not flexible enough was not something anyone pondered too much. In the third revolution (the Internet era), people started considering these questions more. Today, potentially leaving a job over any aspect that doesn't fit with someone's expectations is now a reality for a large part of the workforce. These people are looking for a collection of interesting experiences and the flexibility to live *and* work, not just work *to* live. If you don't keep your top talent motivated and engaged, they'll likely move on to better opportunities in the gig economy, at the start–up next door, or with your biggest competitor.

MIND SWITCH FACT

According to *Doing Good Is Good for You: 2013 Health and Volunteering Study* from UnitedHealth, 87 percent of people who volunteered in the last year said that volunteering had developed teamwork and people skills, and 81 percent agreed that volunteering together strengthens relationships among colleagues. Four out of five employed people who volunteered in the past year say that they feel better about their employer because of the employer's involvement in volunteer activities.

Recently, we were sitting with two friends; one is a baby boomer financial controller in the mining industry, and the other is a millennial team leader of digital initiatives in a large organization. They were talking about the topic of motivating their employees, and the question came up, "How do you motivate a team with a world that changes so fast, especially when the next quarter might be radically different than expected?" The mining industry friend noted that if you have an industry under attack from falling prices and outdated business models, motivating your team is even harder.

Though a difficult, complex question, the answer from our "digital" friend was quite simple: "If you have change happening, everyone needs to get on board and embrace it. You motivate people by making them part of the change and asking them for solutions." They clearly believed that involving the team in the solution was the only path forward. Speaking generally, in past revolutions, the answers were sought from the top. Collaboration and uber-communication are now a feature of healthy workplaces, and dynamic leaders drive toward this goal.

If you are able to motivate your team and peers toward common goals, people who have worked for you and with you will remember how you inspired them toward greater results. They will recognize that you made them want to work harder, reach higher, or do more because they believed in you and respected you. They are also likely to stay longer with the company if they were motivated toward the cause by your example. They will advocate for you and refer talent to you because they are inspired by your energy and beliefs.

"It excites me to work with positive, constructive people who've demonstrated superior initiative, great interpersonal skills, and are committed to furthering their careers."

Motivating others can be difficult—not only due to technological change or lack of clear communication, either. Whether it's corporate bureaucracy, a crummy economy, or your team members are just having a bad day, there are countless factors that will be out of your control. What will always be within your control, however, is how and when you make decisions in order to reach the desired results. Prioritizing your own tasks, delegating work, communicating goals, and motivating teams—all of it is for naught if others can't look to you to make the major decisions when they count the most.

Making the Call

The essence of decision making lies in a trade-off between resources and time spent on one activity or another. Typically, amateur leaders wait too long to make decisions. They study, hem and haw, and analyze ad nauseam. Most delay making choices because they fear they might make the wrong ones or do something in error. The problem with this mindset is obvious: little is accomplished if little is attempted. And little is attempted usually because of fear. When fear of mistakes is magnified, difficulties are magnified, and a vicious cycle is created.

To avoid that cycle, leaders must be decisive early on in any situation. And after they make one decision, then they need to make another, and another, and the next one, and so on. Of course, not all of their decisions are going to be the correct ones. If there was no potential to make a mistake, or if the decision was not difficult in some way, then there would be no decision at all! Whether the end result is good or bad, at least these leaders had the guts to go for it.

> **"Be decisive. Right or wrong. The road is paved with flat squirrels who couldn't make a decision."**

When you are faced with a number of options from which to choose, you need to consider immediate outcomes and the overall impact on the business. Make sure you always think about the future, not just the present. When you are first offered a leadership position, you may get a rush of exhilaration from the idea of being able to say yes or no and make things happen. We guarantee that this feeling won't last. Once the reality of what it means to make game-changing decisions sets in—especially the impact your decisions have today and tomorrow—the realization of the importance and weight of your decisions may also initially take you out of your comfort zone.

Leaders make hundreds of tiny decisions every day, and they add up quickly. They could be decisions to say, or not say, something, to spend time on strategy or on branding, to walk down the hall to see the finance team instead of e-mailing them, to move faster on an announcement than initially agreed, or to ride a bike home instead of catching the train. Some of these choices may seem insignificant, but like it or not, when you are in a leadership role, your team observes and analyzes *every* decision at some level. They are looking for signals on your mood, intentions, wants, and sore points. These seemingly small decisions matter because others rely on your example. And of course the larger decisions matter, too, because they can change the course of companies, careers, and lives.

Just consider the size and importance of the decision that U.S.-based CVS faced when it stopped selling cigarettes—a move estimated to have cost the company more than $1 billion in sales—it was broadly reported to be a $2 billion revenue item. Yet strategically it was what its leaders had to do to position CVS as a healthcare company. The decision made CVS a "first mover" and demonstrated that it cared more than the next drugstore about its image and culture. Not all of us will face such huge decisions on a daily basis, but the principles remain the same—care more, do your homework, and then own your decision. In many ways, it comes down to your mindset.

"Not deciding is also deciding."

The Decision-Making Mindset

You need to accept the fact there is a world of uncertainties out there. You have to consciously and deliberately scrutinize every argument, prediction, alternative, and probable outcome of your action, and then—all on your own—make the decision. Lots of factors inhibit good decisions: stored memories, emotions, relationships, self-interests, biases, and misleading information, not to mention the pressure of time, deadlines, and schedules. You therefore must have the right mindset to combat these potential problems.

Don't make any major decisions when you are tired, mad, sad, sick, or pressured. If you are in any such state and feel you emotionally have the answer, you should still give it more thought. Just one day of getting through whatever is making things seem impossible to resolve can change everything. Similarly, when leaders are stressed or they feel they are out of their depth, they revert to making decisions about the things that make them most comfortable. They will often focus on minutia, becoming distracted by things that are seemingly urgent but arguably *not* important. Don't be that leader. Handling stress is part of a leader's job and is no excuse for bad decisions or, even worse, no decisions.

The decision-making mindset includes the knowledge that you can always change your mind. Usually, when you make a mistake, it's typically due to a lack of information. When you gain more information to cast light on the situation, whether from a conversation, customer feedback, or social media—that's why you have a phone—you should be comfortable in admitting you made the wrong choice, then be ready to fix it and move on. This is where dynamic leaders shine—recovering from mistakes.

In the early 1970s, Debra's friend Jim McBride sat in a garage with Steve Jobs and Steve Wozniak talking about their invention. The two had asked Jim to come over to look at their computer "contraption" and see if he'd be interested in helping them market it. Years later, Jim said, "I couldn't understand what they had. It was beyond me who'd want it. Right then I said 'no,' I'm not interested. I did recommend that whatever they did with it, they better make it damn interesting to people." Jim wasn't afraid of a challenge—after that meeting he moved to the Soviet Union to do sales and marketing for a start-up software company—he just chose another path.

Many people may see Jim's decision as a mistake, but he views it quite differently. Recently Debra asked Jim, "Do you regret your decision?" He said, "Sure, the money would have been nice. But, no, I don't regret it because those two were just too crazy to work with." (And don't chastise Jim for calling Jobs crazy; Steve himself said, "The ones crazy enough to think that they can change the world are the ones who do.") Jim is not only comfortable with his decision, he's happy with it. He's had a highly successful career, and his decision-making mindset and abilities have played a major role in his achievements.

The Decision-Making Process

There is both an art and science to decision making, and perfectly blending the two is a key determinant between good and exceptional leadership. First and foremost, understanding what decisions *you* need to make and which ones other people can make is imperative for survival and, more important, successful leadership—that's right, we're talking about prioritization and delegation. If you don't manage your priorities carefully, and spend your time on the most important decisions, nothing will get done. Trust your team to make good judgments as well. You must appropriately weigh the "urgent and important" decisions and treat them accordingly. Sometimes important decisions take longer to make, but the extra investment of time is worth it. Of course you need to be decisive, and sometimes at breakneck speed, but don't let fast be your only mode.

Good decision making includes the use of all data available but also requires instinct and wisdom, pattern recognition, and people implications—the way a decision affects your team matters a lot. Knowing your blind spots, drawing input from many corners (not just your inner circle),

> **"You make decisions so quickly, you do it on your way to the bathroom while I can agonize over a decision for weeks and still want to change my mind."**

and developing the ability to provide new perspectives will help you in this process. Fresh information, objective analysis, and constructive debate all counter potential problems. After "doing your homework" and weighing your options, you have to provide clear outcomes to your team so your people can rally behind them, even if they were initially skeptical. As mentioned, communication is integral, so while you're making any important decision, clearly and consistently explain why.

When it comes to the most important choices, only explicitly decide on issues that you believe are going to stick. Look for both affirming and contrary signals about any decision, and do not bring your own baggage to the process. Collect the right information, and don't make hubristic decisions based on your own personal preferences. In this process, you will help those you lead unblock and free them to innovate and develop on their own. And helping your team succeed will only further your success.

Mind Switch on Prioritizing

It's not your job to put the brakes on but to give more horsepower. When you decide, delegate, and motivate, assume your people are smart, capable, and you can trust them. It's not asking them where they want to go and taking them there; it's asking questions, then choosing between the long, slow pain or short, sharp pain of deciding. Clearly define their functions and duties. It's okay to give an order. It's okay to say please as long as you show you are good with their motive. With careful consideration, command and control the directive with, "This is what I want; this is what I don't want." Before, during, and after, minimize the emotional impact of problems; always protect your people from unnecessary melodramatic strife. Remember, they are on your team.

Irrespective of whether you identify as a directive leader that likes to keep a tight rein on the team or a laissez-faire leader that likes to leave the space to create between starting and finishing a project, your job is to rank priorities for the team. In a diverse and tech-fueled world, the ability to make good, clear, and rational prioritization and delegation decisions will mean the difference between those around you being happy or harried.

STORIES FROM THE ROAD

Michael Blumstein, CFO at Oak Hill Advisors and former director of U.S. equity research for Morgan Stanley, writes about making decisions and motivating in times of change.

The outlook for equity research was darkening quickly in 2000. Investors, regulators, and the media were all questioning the integrity, credibility, even competence of sell-side analysts, while loose-lipped companies were clamming up due to the SEC's new Reg FD, and the red-hot technology sector was cooling fast. Thus our department was facing true challenges when after 15 years as a financial services sector analyst, I became the U.S. research director at Morgan Stanley in early 2000.

My view was that sell-side research could survive, even thrive, if we delivered real value to our buy-side (asset management) clients. But with each of our 50 lead analysts in essence running his/her own franchise, the test was collectively defining value and executing a strategy so that as a group we could salvage then enhance our reputation, thus stabilizing then growing our revenue stream.

Thinking hard about our clients' needs, my thesis was that analysts should focus on "proprietary, anticipatory, money-making content" and tiered client service—eliminating any semblance of reporting (leave that to $1-a-copy newspapers) and the traditional shotgun approach to marketing (talk to any-one who would pick up the phone).

With the research department numbering 350 (and ulti-mately growing to 575), my first focus was buy-in from the top so that we could scale the effort. That meant in-depth conver-sations with each senior analyst. Fortunately, after some intense give-and-take, our thought leaders were supportive—despite, in some cases, their own uncertainty about how to retool.

To execute, we used a carrot and stick approach. We celebrated our successes loudly. Analysts would articulate the thrill of developing and delivering exclusive work at our monthly department meeting. Meantime, I penned a monthly publication, "In Case You Missed It." It highlighted our most proprietary content, and we distributed it internally as well as to our clients.

We also set barriers to business as usual. We flat out denied airtime at the morning meeting (critical for communicating with salespeople) to analysts who still wanted to comment on company earnings or announcements. We also refused to print routine reports, offering electronic distribution only. At year-end, we specifically evaluated analysts on the value of their content, letting a few go when they couldn't remake their product after a two-year grace period.

Also important, we put up significant money for analysts to produce the research we wanted. After the tech bubble burst, we were watching every dollar of spending (we half-joked about unscrewing every second lightbulb). But we approved virtually every request for proprietary surveys, outside consultants, and specialized data sets that would separate our research from the noise produced elsewhere.

Two years later, the results were in. In 2002—and again in 2003 and 2004—Morgan Stanley's U.S. research ranked number one in the Greenwich Associates annual poll of leading brokerage firms. Challenges remained, but we had righted the ship and were sailing proudly.

<-->

10

MANAGING CONFLICT AND HANDLING CONTROVERSY

Throughout this book, we've discussed the key traits, behaviors, attitudes, and actions that contribute to great leadership. We've also touched on obstacles you'll encounter in any leadership role and how to overcome them. In this final chapter, we go a step further to explicitly cover two challenges that every contemporary leader needs to be prepared for: managing conflict and handling controversy. Both require leaders' willingness to be accountable in difficult situations, even if they aren't the ones to blame. Accountability lies at the heart of leadership, not

> **"Like honesty, true accountability is rarer than it should be."**

only delivering on the results you signed up for, but also taking ownership when things go wrong.

Accountable leaders understand that "accountability" may mean something different to people from various cultures or with diverse experiences or backgrounds. As a leader, you must set a tone for what "accountability" is in your business environment and communicate that clearly to your team. If you're like one former CEO of the bankrupted Enron, who, when asked about the company's finances, said, "I am not an accountant," you're obviously not setting a good example to those around you (who thinks *that* is a reasonable response from the CEO of a company that has just arguably ruined lives?). True blue leaders are trusted and trustworthy and never face such situations.

> **"Don't blame others, and don't make excuses. Take the blame even if it isn't all yours. Give yourself no excuses or reasoning to squirm out of a difficult place. I know what's going on, and if I see your take differs from what I see, I'll believe what I see and not what you tell me."**

Denial is the antithesis of leadership. Irrespective of whether you run a project, a program, a department, or a company, at some level, it is your responsibility to take ownership for all aspects of it. In the words of a chief human resources officer (CHRO) friend of ours, "To be able to do your job, you need to be willing to lose your job," because when situations or people act against your interest—and at some point they will—you still have to own the end result, no matter the conflict or controversy involved.

Managing Conflict

If you are uncomfortable managing conflict, your leadership journey is going to be a tough one. Your innate stance on dealing with conflict is usually an outcome of the environments you have been exposed to during your career and your socialization as a child. While embracing conflict can be learned, unfortunately so can the skill of avoiding conflict! In our experience, conflict avoiders can become some of your most challenging team members/peers/bosses of the future. In order to avoid conflict, it's tempting to take the path of least resistance, but that may not lead to the best—or even good—outcomes. Choosing to learn to *manage* conflict in the spirit of better outcomes is key to success. In that case, you don't have to either embrace or avoid—just learn to manage the situation.

If you hate conflict, and you want everyone to hold hands and sing together, we encourage you to make a mind switch *now*. In the modern workplace, creative tension and strong opinion is almost guaranteed and will contribute to success if dealt with correctly. It's therefore time to start thinking about managing conflict as a subgoal of getting to the heart of the best ideas. Conflict is not something to escape, but to harness.

The only work environment we can imagine that is largely conflict free is where the team is homogenous or ambivalent about what they are doing (or both). The only other place where there is no visible conflict is a dictatorship. As a leader, if you are doing your job correctly—hiring a

> "First thing to understand is that big conflicts are made up of little conflicts. It's like a circuit board. Looking at the whole is complicated, but piece by piece it's easy to connect it all."

diverse workforce, embracing multigenerational teams, and trying to build something great—your work environment will be a hotbed of potential conflict.

Michael Eisner, former CEO and chairman of Disney, described this situation at Disney during an interview at ABC headquarters: "The whole business starts with ideas, and we're convinced that ideas come out of an environment of supportive conflict, which is synonymous with appropriate friction." In describing this concept of appropriate friction for Disney, Eisner referred to the method leaders used to sort through ideas for films at their internal "gong show," which was apparently held weekly. Anyone could share an idea, and only the best survived the group critique. Understandably, meetings where ideas are either supported or killed off can be daunting, and many in the workplace won't have the confidence to succeed in an environment like this. But the creative outcomes of crowdsourcing ideas are an increasingly popular way to get good ideas to be bubbled up to the surface. Eisner mentions, in the same interview, that the idea for *The Little Mermaid* came out of a gong show. Let's face it, many children's lives have been enhanced by *The Little Mermaid*!

When you think about conflict in this context, it feels necessary for success. Supportive, or "good," conflict that enables ideas to flourish irrespective of their source is focused on achieving a company or organizational goal, and how to get there. Bad conflict is that which does not contribute to any sort of progress or success and acts as a productivity and time suck. Petty squabbles about the font on a PowerPoint presentation deck, for example, are not going to help your team or company reach its highest potential. Nor will dragging up and arguing about past events. But conflict over the way to operationalize a breakthrough idea that came from the most junior person in the room about a new offering for the company would be good conflict to have!

Dynamic leaders direct conflict resolution toward priorities. For example, one of Amazon's leadership principles is "Leaders are obligated to respectfully challenge decisions when they disagree, even when doing so is uncomfortable or exhausting. Leaders have conviction and are tenacious. They do not compromise for the sake of social cohesion. Once a decision is determined, they commit wholly." (https://www.amazon.jobs/principles) Amazon CEO Jeff Bezos emphasizes success through conflict over blindly seeking social cooperation or harmony. Though this tactic might not work for all leaders, we applaud Bezos's guts and his willingness to manage conflict, bucking social connections or niceties when necessary, to get results.

MIND SWITCH FACT

Fast Company notes in an article about using conflict to your benefit that a 2010 study by VitalSmarts, in Provo, Utah, found that 95 percent of employees have trouble voicing differences of opinion, which results in a loss of roughly $1,500 per eight-hour workday in lost productivity.

(July 2014, "How to Use Conflict to Your Advantage at Work")

The Three Steps of Conflict Management

Conflict can be triggered by activities around small or large goals, but as long as it is handled productively, your team and you will be okay. If conflict is about what someone said, how he did something, or what he thinks about topics unrelated to any stated goal, then bad conflict is looming on the horizon and must be mitigated.

Whether good or bad, in our view, there are three steps to managing conflict that have consistently worked for us when leading and operating in fast-moving business environments. We could debate good and bad conflict boundaries forever, but whatever the root cause, our view on handling them remains the same. The three steps we suggest are:

1. **Remove the oxygen from the situation.** Emotions rarely improve a situation, whether financial, operational, or team related. Like fires, business challenges usually grow when given air. We find this principle helpful in making sure that we always quickly get to the core of an issue and don't let drama or emotional responses take over.

2. **Be generous.** Strange situations arise in every business. (For example, an employee of a large company once decided that setting up a small business in a spare conference room during lunch hour, then bringing in other employees to help manage and earn some money on the side, wouldn't harm anyone.) Jumping to conclusions about who was responsible and why people did what they did rarely helps find a positive path forward. Being generous and assuming that a person's intent was honorable, despite the outcome, is a good starting point. Generosity for us extends to (a) giving the benefit of the doubt at the outset, (b) giving liberal feedback on where someone could have taken a different course of action, and (c) being willing to wipe the slate clean (at least once) if the situation is resolved appropriately.

3. **Share context.** People are more reasonable in their reaction if they are given a more complete picture, or fuller context, for why a certain activity (or lack of activity!) caused conflict. Too often, we hear overreactions to situations that seemingly blindside us. Such situations might include declines in business activity, unauthorized budget expenditures, product quality issues, or any other manner of activities that make a business such a fascinating ecosystem. Sharing the context of a difficult situation with the rest of the team involved and describing the conditions that led to the situation provides a way for everyone to learn from mistakes. For example, a team misses one month of their revenue target and their boss goes crazy about it in a team meeting, which causes a lot of conflict as people try to defend their activity. The context might be that every other division missed their revenue target also and now people have to be let go. Context is a great leveler, and it always matters.

MIND SWITCH FACT

A 2008 study by consulting firm CPP found the primary causes of workplace conflict are seen as personality clashes and warring egos (49 percent), followed by stress (34 percent) and heavy workloads (33 percent). Culture also plays a part in the perception of causes and differs across geographies: Brazilian workers are more likely to see a clash of values as a major cause of conflict (24 percent). In France, 36 percent of employees saw a lack of honesty as a key factor, compared with a global average of 26 percent.

Unsurprisingly, poorly managed conflicts have a cost attached to them: the average employee spends 2.1 hours a week dealing with conflict. For the United States alone, that translates to 385 million working days spent every year as a result of conflict in the workplace. One in six (16 percent) say a recent dispute escalated in duration and/ or intensity, and only 11 percent of those surveyed have never experienced a disagreement that escalated.

(*Global Human Capital Report*, July 2008)

As a leader, practicing conflict management starts with listing the people in your workplace who make you uncomfortable for some reason, objectively diagnosing why you are uncomfortable with them, and working on that issue. At the core, it will usually be because (1) you sense they disagree with you on something or (2) they don't like you. On the first, get used to it if you want to work in passionate and successful environments, and on the latter, just know that trying to be liked as a leader is folly. Your goal as a leader should not be to be "liked" but to lead the organization, team, or project to the stated goals. Many leaders are likeable, but don't mix this up with good leaders valuing "being liked."

You must get comfortable with how others perceive your willingness to engage when conflict arises. To do so, ask your team for 360-degree feedback on your ability to manage conflict situations. It is an area where your own view of your actions and the perception of others can vary dramatically. Until you understand any gaps, it is hard to put the right practice into place.

Next, learn to use the two simple words "I understand" when in any conflict situation. It will keep you from saying,

"I agree" or "I disagree" before you are sure where you stand on any situation. It also reduces the likelihood of further inflaming a situation. Per step one earlier in this section, taking the oxygen out of any situation is paramount to resolving the conflict, and potentially benefiting from healthy debate, but once you start getting into agree/disagree language there is a tendency for conflict to escalate.

At the beginning of the chapter, we mentioned that managing conflict is something that can be learned. We believe this to be 100 percent true, but only *if* the desire to be a great leader is also present. If you are a conflict avoider at your core, your desire to be a great leader must have a stronger gravitational pull than your desire to escape a situation when conflict arises. This is important because the frequency and reasons for conflict in a workplace can be high, often petty, and very costly. You will face conflict regularly throughout your leadership journey, and learning to grow from it and move on fast once it is resolved is key to staying positive and making the best decisions. It will also help you in handling the inevitable controversy you will face, both individually and as a leader of an organization.

Handling Controversy

Controversy often comes with conflict, but not always. Controversy can arise in the form of a PR scandal, an HR scandal, or a random act that causes you to reconsider the potential range of outcomes you thought possible—these situations are often referred to as "black swans." Black swan events are typically random and unexpected. The ability to react with grace when controversy arrives is a pinnacle leadership attribute. Reacting with the type of kindly confidence we spoke of in Chapter 2 will lead to good outcomes in otherwise bad situations, where you look back and are proud of the way you handled them. Such reactions are usually hard won and only achieved through preparation and with the support of a great team.

The idea that leaders know what is going on in their departments, companies, or teams before the rest of their employees, however, is no longer a practical standpoint. This makes preparing for bad situations more difficult than ever. The speed of information, through channels like instant messaging and social media, will always outpace leaders' knowledge.

> **"Being prepared for the unexpected is part of being a great leader."**

In addition, in the fourth revolution, controversy is more likely than ever because privacy is dead and the workplace is so incredibly diverse. In a twist of irony, controversy can be sparked by the very nature of your diverse workplace, which we have spoken of as so positive throughout this book. As discussed, the number of languages, generations, religious beliefs, and cultural norms that are encountered daily are exploding. In such a world, it is more likely that a couple of your team members will one day approach a problem from widely different perspectives and may clash. Tempers could flare, and regrettable things can be said. Or even worse, a customer complaint may reveal ethical or moral dilemmas that you have never had to deal with before. This is more likely because of the fast tech and demographic changes we are experiencing. Things like using a phone at the table or while on the job are normal. Yet customers and bosses still want full attention. Equality—whether it is based on gender, race, or sexual identity—is a hotter issue than ever, as our diverse society wrestles with how to adapt to demographic change.

While the presence of controversy is a given whenever there is human interaction, the spark for it and the underlying problems that lead to the interaction change in texture and form over time. Controversy around sweatshops is a good example of a relatively old world problem, or, going back further, the ethics around kids working in coal mines is a controversial topic that we could have seen coming. A new world problem might be around the use of drones to identify locations of potential targets for a sales campaign that leads to ethical concerns around privacy. We haven't seen this example yet, but as regulation around the use of drones is being determined across the world, such items are sure to arise.

Controversy can be complicated and involve multiple people in a chain of actions. Sometimes it can come in the simplest form of a rogue e-mail that goes to unintended audiences—this one is going to happen to us, so we might as well be ready for it. The most common way this happens is when you "reply all" with a comment that was meant for only one person and the content of the e-mail you are replying with is provocative or even inflammatory (at worst!). We are all aware that the functionality in our e-mail systems to "retrieve" an e-mail is not effective. The only way to avoid these e-mail snafus is to be high integrity at all times and never say anything you would regret later. The truth is, however, that others will still do controversial things that directly or indirectly implicate you in leadership.

A Human Response

As a leader, if *you* are the source of controversy, your first point of defense is honesty. Always. The second step is owning up to your mistakes and maintaining accountability for your errors. It is almost embarrassing for us to write this because the following advice is so simple, yet every day, these principles are broken by leaders, hurting their careers and performance and leaving their teams disappointed:

>> Don't send out a message to your colleagues that you wouldn't want your mother, father, or favorite aunt to read.

>> Never e-mail salary information or other personal information without encrypting it or protecting it with a password.

>> Don't have an affair in the workplace. You *will* get caught.

>> Never use company resources in a way that the most innocent of your team members would not approve of. (Your own lens on using company resources may have migrated over your career—using another's lens when you are thinking about such matters is a more evolved way of leading.)

When you are not the source of the controversy, you have two options: (1) get on the front foot or (2) sit in graceful silence. In our view, the nature of the controversy (legal, ethical, or physical) and who was harmed will determine which way you should react. If your company or team is at the center of the issue, it is hard to think of a situation where the front foot would not be the way to handle it.

If you or your organization is on the edges of the controversy (e.g., an industry scandal), sitting in graceful silence might be the way to show that you intend to recover through business as usual. This second approach is extraordinarily hard, and in our experience will be much criticized at the time, but in the spirit of keeping a calm and orderly environment, it may be the right way forward.

The shortest possible answer to how to handle controversy is to use very *human* means of resurrecting any mishaps, even if machines led to the error—for example, a car braking system causes an accident. A town hall, an in-person explanation, a vulnerable and honest confession is always best. Don't send another e-mail to try to resolve it. It takes more guts to stand up in person and own it—that is what leaders do.

Keep in mind, the truth is always going to come out. When controversy inevitably rears its ugly head, get to the bottom of the situation fast and repair it tirelessly. As with many other aspects or leadership, make sure to stay generous and kindly confident when handling controversies. Don't assume intentions of the people involved—employees or colleagues—were bad when controversy breaks, just get the facts and start to make a plan to remedy the problem.

While focusing in on a solution, don't use a blowtorch to bake the cake—get all the right people in the room, calmly talk about the extent of the damage, and choose a path or solution that matches the severity of the situation. You can always call in the "big guns"—the people in charge of the governance of the company or the project leaders—later if you have underestimated the severity in your first analysis.

The Mind Switch on Managing Conflict and Controversy

Bad people don't make good leaders. While the workforce is full of good people, there are also lots of people who have to learn to be good enough. Leadership is about action and example. Be generous of spirit when dealing with conflict and controversy because you have to remember that anything can be taken out of context. Always address behavior, not character or motive. Talk about everything as behavior. You must set the example and instruct the behavior you want and be rigid about it. You have to make tough choices or people won't respect you. All problems if not easily solved go up the ladder and get solved by better-quality people. Be the better-quality leader.

STORIES FROM THE ROAD

Chris and Tara Seegers, who own Hillside, Colorado (www.townofhillside.com), write about communicating across generations.

We bought a town . . . now what?

My wife and I are both entrepreneurs with a passion for real estate. In our late twenties (not long ago), we purchased a small, historic town in southern Colorado. Our vision was to collaborate with local residents to renovate and reinvigorate the community in a spirit of "People First, Then Profit." We wanted to create an environment where everyone who experienced the town, or interacted with our business, would leave with a net positive experience.

We realized this to be a lofty goal, one that prioritized employee and customer relationships above short-term gain, and our convictions were soon tested. Approximately a year into the project we received a call from our town manager informing us of her resignation. She stated that she was no longer interested in working with us, which we found to be a puzzler, as we believed that our employee/employer relationship was going quite well . . . little did we know!

Our manager was in her early sixties and had overseen the town for more than 20 years. During her tenure she had assumed many roles, including postmistress, store clerk, and property manager, and had performed each role with a strong desire to see the community prosper. She cared deeply for her community, and we believed there to be an alternative motivation for the resignation.

During this time I was reading the book *How to Win Friends and Influence People*, which presented me with two important realizations: *1. Relationships are everything. 2. Listen, and then listen some more.* Guided by those truths, we listened to our manager communicate the variety of reasons that her employment situation simply couldn't work anymore. As she expressed her concerns, we realized that all of them pertained to job functions that utilized technology we had recently implemented. It was *technology* that was the key issue, not any of the other reasons she had cited. Being of a younger generation, we had viewed the technology as simple and intuitive and hadn't appreciated the generational differences that left our manager feeling inadequate and stressed.

Soon thereafter, we created and agreed upon a solution that both advanced the business and kept her in the job she loved. Each generation has tremendous value coupled with areas of struggle, but we believe people are absolutely worth the extra effort. Compassionate listening paired with innovative problem solving sure goes a long way.

Conclusion

GETTING RESULTS

Getting results is the culmination of the leadership and management behaviors, attitudes, and actions discussed throughout the book. Of course, "results" aren't a skill you can practice, like hosting meetings, or a subject you can study up on, such as compensation. Results to one leader might be strictly financial—everything else is just "fluff"—while to another they might be a complex, triple bottom line outcome where social, environmental, and financial impacts all matter. For yet others, the idea of results is in the beauty of the product or service delivered, and they expect the economics to take care of themselves. We have seen leaders that express all three of these philosophies and everything in between!

In our experience, the best way to think about results is as the final destination of a long journey. There are short, medium, and long-term milestones that will occur because of the decisions you make as a leader. The long-term results are the most important because they are the ones that will have the most impact and help you develop more leaders for the future.

Results orientation is not a bent that every leader naturally has, but making the leadership mind switches we suggest throughout can help every potential leader get to good results in the fourth revolution. Being results-oriented is a good thing.

It keeps you centered as a leader and motivates those around you. It stops the meandering along random product and service journeys that can take over in any growing organization and keeps everyone aligned around a tangible outcome.

In our experience, the best leaders have a simple framework for how they think about results: for example, revenue, client satisfaction, profitability, or new customers. People can't remember a plethora of measures of success. This doesn't mean you can't have great analytics and metrics that you use to judge different little bits of the business, but the best leaders don't force their teams and employees to try to remember them all.

To decide what results to use as your most important measure of success, first look at your company's goals. Unless you are the CEO, you will probably have a subset of results that are firmly in your control. Write all of these down. Highlight the ones that are *most* controllable. Then checkmark the one that you think will most likely make the biggest difference in the medium term (one to three years). This is the one you should start socializing with your team as the collective goal.

Getting business results is usually a lot murkier than winning or losing. It is almost guaranteed that if you set a numerical goal for your team to hit, you will either over- or undershoot it—it is the nature of predicting future outcomes. You must also understand that as a dynamic leader in a world of constant change, there is more to getting results than setting a target and letting the team go. You have to communicate widely and comprehensively and redirect them when there is confusion.

The most important thing to realize about the results you deliver, however, is that they matter greatly, not only to your team, company, or industry, but to the world around you.

Today's onslaught of technological changes in the workplace has made both managing and leading more complex, and you'll have to steer your way through the maze successfully and tactfully. The idea that mountains of data can now drive good decisions is key to this complexity and will only continue to grow in the future. Intuition used to be an advantage in the workplace because it was hard to prove a concept within a reasonable time frame and budget. You just had to rely on wisdom and experience, then go for it. This is no longer the case. Today, you need to be adept at handling ambiguity, speed, technology, a changing workforce, a more global atmosphere, and all the intricacies that are inherent in these issues.

The demographic changes in the workforce have added to its vibrancy. We can no longer think of management strategies in a general sense. There is no "average" response to situations. We've said it before: leaders need to be nimble enough to lead across generations and styles. The world has changed such that the melting pot of views, reactions, and potential outcomes is vast. Leading in this environment is like competing in the modern pentathlon—you have to be agile and adaptable, mostly mentally, but sometimes physically, too!

Throughout the book, we have been talking about the context behind why the world has changed for leaders and why you must adapt. The premise has been that we need to embrace the technological and demographic changes that are upon us. Having a view on each of these topics is critical because you are going to be asked for your view and you will be expected to deliver on it as you develop as a fourth generation leader. Keep in mind the four leadership qualities that you will need: to be true blue, kindly confident, enlightened, and tenacious. And the four behaviors you will need to exhibit: to be uber-communicative, dynamic, playful, and unblocking. And success will come easier to you.

Let us leave you with this last bit of advice: you will find success in whatever you do if you remember that everybody has the right to pursue happiness and needs to love, to be loved, and to laugh. Then direct your actions toward helping them pursue their dreams while you also pursue yours. So let's make the mind switch and get ready for the next revolution.

《《《〉》》》

Now is the time for you to share your "stories from the road" with us. We want *The Leadership Mind Switch* to open up the conversations in your team, your company, and with your friends. We don't pretend to have all the answers, but we certainly are looking for them. Together, with your help, we will achieve that goal.

Contact us at:

www.makethemindswitch.com
www.debrabenton.com
www.kyliewf.com

Acknowledgments

FROM DEBRA

Thank you to my husband, Rodney Sweeney, for supporting and helping in all my endeavors. And to my family and friends starting with Curtis Rex Carter, Emma and Killian Williams, Samantha and Madelyn Weinstein, Savannah and Cutter Schorre, Chelsea and Blake Harrison, Pamela Cook, Joyce Dixon, Megan Richardson Campos, and Inge Trump. These people make every day an easy day for me.

FROM KYLIE

Thank you to my immediate and extended circle of family and friends. Especially my husband, Adam, for the inspiration and cheering along the way, our kids, Finn, Alannah, and Kierah, my wonderful colleagues, former colleagues, clients, and friends. Thanks to my sister-in-law Natalie and dear friends Britta and Alex who were always there for me. Big thanks also go to my father, who reminded me that if you think you are leading but turn around and no one is following, you are really just out for a walk. You all make life exceptional to me.

FROM BOTH OF US

Thank you to the pros at McGraw-Hill, and especially our fearless editors, Cheryl Ringer and Zachary Gajewski. Also to our contributors to stories from the road; Mike, Kristi, Margaret, Bob, Christopher, Meredith, Tom, Sharon, Susan, Jose, Eliza, Dean, Cheryl, Chris and Tara, Alyssa, and Sorcha.

Further Resources

Books

Eric Ries, *The Lean Startup* (New York: Crown Business, 2011).

Ruma Bose and Lou Faust, *Mother Teresa, CEO* (New York: MJF Books, 2011).

General Stanley McChrystal with Tantum Collins, Chris Fussel, and David Silverman, *Team of Teams* (New York: Penguin Publishing Group, 2015).

Kelly Leonard and Tom Yorton, *Yes, And* (New York: HarperCollins Publishers, 2015).

Douglas Conant and Mette Norgaard, *TouchPoints* (San Francisco: Jossey-Bass, 2011).

Robert M. Gates, *Duty* (New York: Alfred A. Knopf, 2014).

Peggy Noonan, *Simply Speaking* (New York: HarperCollins Publishers, 1998).

Russel B. Reynolds, *The Officer's Guide* (Harrisburg: The Stackpole Co., 1967).

Peggy Noonan, *What I Saw at the Revolution* (London: Random House Trade Paperback, 1990).

Klaus Schwab, *The Fourth Industrial Revolution* (Schwab, 2016).

Margaret Heffernan, *Beyond Measure* (Simon and Schuster, 2015).

Guy Kawasaki, *Enchantment* (Penguin, 2012).

Reid Hoffman and Ben Casnocha, *The Start-up of You* (Crown Business Books, 2012).

Andy Stefanovich, *Look at More* (Jossey-Bass, 2011).

Ron A. Carucci and Eric C. Hansen, *Rising to Power* (Greenleaf Book Group Press, 2014).

Jason Fried and David Heinemeier Hansson, *Rework* (Crown Business, 2010).

Daniel H. Pink, *Drive* (Penguin Group, 2009).

Alan S. Berson and Richard G. Stieglitz, *Leadership Conversations* (Jossey-Bass, 2013).

Daniel Goleman, Richard Boyatzis, and Annie McKee, *Primal Leadership* (Boston: Harvard Business School Press, 2004).

Anne Lamott, *Bird by Bird* (New York: Pantheon Books, 1994).

Henry Chesbrough, Livescience.com, *Open Innovation*.

Jeffrey Pfeffer, *Leadership BS: Fixing Workplaces and Careers One Truth at a Time* (Harper Collins, 2015).

Magazines

William Finnegan, "The Man Who Wouldn't Sit Down," *The New Yorker*, October 5, 2015, 40–51.

Jiayang Fan, "The Accused," *The New Yorker*, October 12, 2015, 42–50.

Rebecca Mead, "The Couture Club," *The New Yorker*, September 21, 2015, 76–87.

"The Disrupters," *Vanity Fair*, October 2015, 192–219.

Amy Davidson, "Paging Dr. Carson," *The New Yorker*, September 14, 2015.

Jason Fried, "Nailing the Next Five Years," *INC.*, September 2014, 145.

Leigh Buchanan, "How I Did It," *INC.*, July/August 2014, 77–78.

"Laughing Matter," Weightwatchers.com, May/June 2015, 25–26.

David Berreby, "How Humans Can Bind Groups Together and Tear Nations Apart," *Korn Ferry Briefings*, August 11, 2014, 40–45.

Macc Andreesen, "Push Back," *The New Yorker*, May 18, 2015, 64.

Mark Graham," Rosewood Rising," *Departures*, September 9, 2015.

Ray Kelly, "Necessary Luxury," *Departures*, September 9, 2015.

Christopher Mims, "Meet Venture Capital's Teenage Analyst," *Wall Street Journal*, October 18, 2015.

Tim Harford, "The Power of Saying No," *The Undercover Economist*, February 11, 2015.

Korn Ferry Briefings, The Optimism/Pessimism Issue, volume 5, 2015.

Index

About the Authors

Debra Benton is a globally recognized executive coach (ranked in the top 10 coaches in the world and the number one female coach by www.topCEOcoaches.com), bestselling award-winning business author of 10 books, and popular conference keynote speaker on leadership and executive effectiveness. Benton has been a successful business owner for many years having started her first company in 1976 at the age of 23, and over those years has conducted assignments in 18 countries. She has written for *Harvard Business Review*, the *Wall Street Journal, Bloomberg Businessweek,* and *Fast Company.* She is regularly sought out as an expert resource on leadership issues for those publications as well as CNN, CBS, and NBC talk shows. Her parents ran their own businesses, and she grew up listening about work-related issues around the dinner table from the time she was in kindergarten. She says that she learned from her parents "not only how to make a living but how to live."

www.debrabenton.com

Kylie Wright-Ford is a C-level executive, board member, speaker, entrepreneur, avid traveler, and farmer. Born and raised in Cowra, a small town in Australia, she has lived and worked on three continents and now lives in Atlanta, Georgia, USA. Kylie was most recently the chief operating  and strategy officer for World 50, a company that exists to connect executives with their peers for conversations about topics like leadership, sustainability, global politics, and how to keep up with digital innovation. Prior to World 50, Kylie worked for New York–based GLG, the world's largest professional learning platform. She completed her MBA at Oxford University in 2005 after working in finance in Australia for 10 years including for Goldman Sachs JBWere. Kylie studied economics at the University of New England in Armidale and completed Honors at the University of Melbourne. She has two children with her Australian husband Adam Ford and still calls Australia home.

www.kyliewf.com

Essential Executive Guides from Bestselling Author D.A. Benton

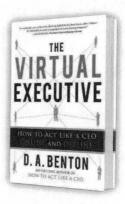

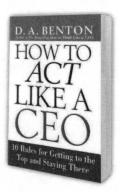